D0500072

Praise for

NOVEL ADVICE

"In Jay Bushman's delightful *Novel Advice*, Aunt Antigone dishes out sage counsel for some of the people who need it most: literary characters. Whether she's giving marriage tips to Lady Macbeth or counseling Long John Silver on how to manage his money, Aunt Antigone is funny, wry, and sometimes surprisingly wise."

—Sean Stewart, Emmy winner and New York Times *bestselling author of* Cathy's Book

"In *Novel Advice*, Jay Bushman combines his quick wit and kind heart in the persona of Aunt Antigone to create a source of sage advice for those struggling with a wide variety of problems, be they literary or literal."

—Margaret Dunlap, writer and co-executive producer of The Lizzie Bennet Diaries

"If you're looking for a book to make you laugh out loud and uplift your spirit then you need to read Jay Bushman's *Novel Advice*—like right now. Charming, thoughtful, and clever, the book brings to life the trials and tribulations of some of the world's most beloved literary characters through the framework of an agony aunt column you have to read to believe. It's awesome!"

—Amber Benson, actress, Buffy the Vampire Slayer

"An inventive story and a loving tribute to literary tradition! I expect nothing less from Jay Bushman!"

—Bernie Su, three-time Emmy-winning storyteller and co-creator of The Lizzie Bennet Diaries

"Jay Bushman's *Novel Advice* is an absolute delight! A literary guessing game with great life advice to boot. This is the most fun the Western Canon has been in ages."

—Kate Rorick, co-author of The Secret Diary of Lizzie Bennet *and* The Epic Adventures of Lydia Bennet

NOVEL ADVICE

PRACTICAL WISDOM *for* YOUR FAVORITE LITERARY CHARACTERS

NOVEL ADVICE

PRACTICAL WISDOM *for* YOUR FAVORITE LITERARY CHARACTERS

JAY BUSHMAN

TILLER PRESS

New York London Toronto Sydney New Delhi

An Imprint of Simon & Schuster, Inc.
1230 Avenue of the Americas
New York, NY 10020

First Tiller Press hardcover edition November 2020

TILLER PRESS and colophon are trademarks of Simon & Schuster, Inc.

For information about special discounts for bulk purchases, please contact Simon & Schuster Special Sales at 1-866-506-1949 or business@simonandschuster.com.

The Simon & Schuster Speakers Bureau can bring authors to your live event. For more information or to book an event, contact the Simon & Schuster Speakers Bureau at 1-866-248-3049 or visit our website at www.simonspeakers.com.

Interior design by Jennifer Chung

Manufactured in the United States of America

10 9 8 7 6 5 4 3 2 1

Library of Congress Cataloging-in-Publication Data has been applied for.

ISBN 978-1-9821-5629-9
ISBN 978-1-9821-5635-0 (ebook)

For my father,
who is alive and well
and living in Sweden

TABLE OF CONTENTS

CHAPTER 3: RECEIVING AN EDUCATION

CHAPTER 4: BODY, MIND, AND SPIRIT

CHAPTER 5: BONDS OF MATRIMONY

CHAPTER 6: THE WAY WE WORK

CHAPTER 7: MONEY MATTERS

CHAPTER 8:
COMMUNITY AND SOCIETY

CHAPTER 9:
ENDINGS

INTRODUCTION

When faced with the knotty questions of existence, real people have many ways to get help. They turn to friends, counselors, therapists, and—my favorite—advice columnists to guide them through their dilemmas. Does she really love me? Should I go for this promotion? If I make this sacrifice, will it be worth it? Should I bury my brother in defiance of the king's new law?

I never had an "agony aunt" to ask for advice. If I had, maybe things would have turned out better between my uncle Creon and me. But knowing the gods and their capriciousness, probably not. But even if it wouldn't have changed the outcome, it would have been nice to be able to step out of my story for a moment, to share my troubles with someone, to receive counsel that wasn't dependent on the plot or theme or whim of a writer's pen.

Because let's be honest: it's hard to be a fictional character. Everything you do is in support of some master narrative. All of your choices are constrained by the story, genre, form, and the particular skills (or lack thereof) of the storyteller. And whatever you do, your choices are judged, analyzed, mocked, and questioned by readers and critics who just can't wait to catalog your myriad flaws and failures.

But just because readers and writers may know how the stories end doesn't mean that the characters do. While they're in the middle, they have no idea if they're in a comedy or a tragedy, an epic or fable or farce. Are they the hero or the villain, the love interest or the comic sidekick? It doesn't seem quite fair, does it?

Who will be there for the fictional characters? To help them work through their problems, their worries and self-doubt, their aspirations and fears? Who will listen to them with empathy, with understanding that they are trapped in webs made by others, on tracks they can't see toward ends they don't know? Who will help them get where they need to go, without spoiling what comes next?

I will. As a somewhat fictional creation myself, it only seems fitting. So I'll be the agony aunt for the unreal. You can call me "Aunt Antigone."

Chapter 1

YOUNG LOVE

While all romantic relationships are fraught with passion, anxiety, anticipation, yearning, and heartbreak, nothing compares to the foolish, desperate intensity of young lovers.

They tremble with anticipation, unsure of where the boundaries between themselves and their beloveds begin and end. They cannot find the words to express their true feelings, or else they find too many words. Every moment is life and death. Every misunderstanding is a catastrophe. No one has ever felt anything like what they are feeling, and no one will ever again.

It's easy to roll your eyes at their foolishness, their gullibility, their naked need for assurance that they will not be consumed by their emotions. But remember, you too may have once felt like they did. And back in the midst of your juvenile passion, did you ask for help from someone older and wiser in the ways of love? Were they kind? Did they mock you? Or did they tell you some truth that you swore you'd never accept, only later to discover they'd been right all along?

Roll your eyes at the earnest, intense, solipsistic young lovers if you must, but understand that you're really only scoffing at a version of your younger self. And haven't we all suffered through enough heartbreak already?

So be kind, because even the oldest of us can be instantly transported back to our callow youth when struck by Eros's arrow. I can still feel the spot where it first struck me, when I first laid eyes on Haemon. Even after all the tragedy that came after, I'd never want to forget that moment.

Dear Aunt Antigone:

My boyfriend is a pretty big deal. Where we're from, he's well known, well connected, and everybody has an opinion about him. So, we've been trying to keep our relationship private. When we're alone together, everything is great! But whenever the outside world intrudes, our situation becomes completely unbearable. It sometimes feels as if the entire kingdom is trying to tear us apart.

Lately, it's gotten so much worse. He's had to deal with a ton of family drama—his uncle is pretty ruthless. He was expecting a big promotion that, honestly, he was cheated out of. It was all pretty rotten. Then my family found out about us, and I've been getting nonstop lectures from my father and brother about how our relationship will never work, that he's out of my star, that he doesn't have the freedom to marry whom he chooses because of the health of the whole state, blah blah blah. I'm trying not to listen to them, but they're starting to get into my head, and I find myself wondering if they maybe have a point. He really is on a different level than me. He could have anybody he wants. So what makes me special?

Am I a fool for thinking this relationship could last? Why can't everybody leave us alone and let us be happy?

—Green Girl

Dear Green:

It makes sense, given his notoriety and such a toxic environment, that you and your boyfriend would want to keep your relationship to yourselves for as long as possible. In fact, most romantic relationships begin with a period of cocooning, inhabiting a small bubble that is just large enough for the two of you.

That cocoon is cozy, warm, nurturing. In it, there's only you and him. It feels incredible, and naturally you want to stay inside forever and ever. But as much as you want the world to leave you alone, if you stay in a cocoon too long, it becomes a prison. Trapped, you'll dissolve into each other, scratching and clawing for space, for air, for any escape.

Sooner or later, every relationship needs to emerge into the bright light of the outside world. Once there, it will be subjected to never-ending tests and challenges. Family disapproval, competing priorities, mismatched opportunities, and all the other poisons the world has at its disposal. Keeping love alive is difficult enough for two individuals navigating their own hopes, fears, dreams, and self-defeating habits. But when you add outside voices—even well-meaning ones—it gets immeasurably harder.

Is your relationship doomed? Of course not. It's just going to take a lot of work for you and your boyfriend to keep it going. In some ways, every couple faces the same challenges you do. Yours may just play out in a decidedly more public way.

Then there's that part of you that doubts, that wonders if you even deserve him. Lately, that uncertainty speaks to you with the voices of the men in your family. You must know that your father and brother, for all their annoying lectures, are genuinely invested in your well-being. And if your boyfriend's status really is that much more elevated than yours—well there's a long history of men in elevated positions convincing women of their true love, only to abandon them later when their relationship became inconvenient. In these cases, the men feel little consequence while the women pay the full price. I'm not saying that's what's happening in your situation, but only that there's enough of a precedent that your father and brother are not totally unrealistic in their concerns. But only you can decide if their advice rings true. If it doesn't, then I hope that you can honor them for caring about you while you clearly and forcefully tell them to butt out.

On the other hand, if even the tiniest part of you suspects that they might be right, then you need to have a candid conversation with your boyfriend as soon as possible. Because, if you really want your relationship to survive and thrive, it's going to take forging a two-against-the-world alliance. You'll need to find a way to be together where everyone else can see you, where you can hear all the voices telling you that you're doing wrong. And you'll need to find a way to keep them from drowning out what your heart tells you.

Dear Aunt Antigone:

Through a rather peculiar set of circumstances, I found myself forced to share a room—and a bed!—with a stranger whilst boarding in New Bedford. Naturally I was reticent at first, especially after hearing the wildest descriptions of his character from the landlord, including a troubling tale about how he was out "peddling heads." When I first laid eyes on him, I found his manners quite queer and savage—he is covered in tattoos, worships a little wooden idol, and sleeps with his tomahawk. He may even be a cannibal! Surely he's no Christian.

But in spite of all that, I quickly discovered his true nobility. He is a marvel—towering like a mainmast, strong as a grampus, and his head is excellent, phrenologically speaking. On entering a room, all eyes turn to watch him. A loving, affectionate comity has sprung up between us.

I was not seeking a new bosom companion. My only thought was of shipping out on a whaleboat. As fate would have it, my friend is an experienced harpooner, and seeks a similar situation. He has proposed we ship together. My soul soared upon the first thought of extending our unity. We are off to Nantucket, the most promising port for an adventurous whaleman to embark from.

But on the cusp of plunging forward, I find a curious timidity arising. While my splintered heart lifts at the thought of a three-year voyage in his society, is it rash to splice hands with such haste? Is it sensible to distrust this sudden flame of affection? Or am I in the grip of another one of my hypos?

—Call Me Sheepish

Dear Sheepish:

Is there anything better than meeting someone who you instantly connect *with? Language, customs, habits, philosophies can all fall away through a simple, powerful connection between two like-minded souls.*

I would be remiss if I did not point out that the manner in which you describe your new friend, the way you deflect the ogling of his physicality onto others, the "coziness" of your shared domesticity, and even your choice of the word proposed, *all suggest some deeper prodding is necessary to sound the depth of your feelings. But regardless, the central question remains: only knowing a few things about him, can you trust that your blazing affections will last for the duration of your time together? Put another way, can you rely on your feelings about him? Do you have complete trust that he reciprocates your affections? Do you truly know what he's thinking? Are you honestly certain of what he wants? How can you know if you're making the right decision?*

In many ways, this is the problem underlying all others: Who can truthfully interpret what hides behind the mask of a smiling face on your dearest love? What do you need to know, to allow yourself to trust in him utterly? Is there some amount of proof that will ever be enough? You can certainly decide to pursue that evidence, but you may discover the more you find, the more you need, until you are gorged on facts but starved of meaning.

And then you'll have to admit that what you're really after isn't proof, but a guarantee—that you'll be safe, that you won't get hurt this time, that it's all right to be vulnerable. But there are no guarantees, and there never can be. Anybody who tries to tell you they know the absolute truth is peddling false coin.

What you're really searching for is faith, which is by definition trust devoid of proof. To accept that means embracing that other people—and the wide world!—are unfathomable mysteries. You can try to hold fast to some meaning or purpose and hope it doesn't smash you to splinters. Or you can choose to stay loose, and follow where the wind, or your heart, takes you.

Dear Aunt Antigone:

I have this friend, and she thinks she's in love with this one man. But he's clearly not right for her. She is almost certainly a gentleman's daughter—she's my dearest friend, so how can she be anything else?—while he is nothing more than a farmer. A successful farmer, to be sure. But that's all he'll ever be. Meanwhile, there's another man, a gentleman and a clergyman, and thus more befitting of her position. They are meant for each other.

Now, I've had a long track record at excellent matchmaking—no matter what some people who love to find fault with me might say. It is thanks to me that my darling Miss Taylor became Mrs. Weston. Simply put, I just know when people belong together.

And yet, I sense a certain reticence from my friend. I just want the best for her. How can I make her understand that?

—Vexed, Distressed

Dear Vexed:

I generally receive two kinds of letters. The first type comes from a person caught in a dilemma who has looked at all their options and simply needs a nudge to figure out which one is right for them. The other is from someone who knows exactly what they want to do and is looking for some outside authority to give them permission. You, my dear, are clearly of the latter disposition.

You speak like a young person, and while youth should be celebrated, it also sometimes must be endured. I'd like to tell you that you have no business telling this friend to deny her feelings, whether they're for a farmer or a clergyman or anyone else. If she's wrong, it will be her mistake to own. I'd like to tell you that you should focus on your own heart and leave others to theirs. But that's not what you want to hear.

Let's take another angle. Can you imagine yourself in your friend's shoes? Can you imagine that you feel deeply for someone, and then a friend swoops in to tell you that you're wrong? And proceeds to badger, cajole, and bully you into believing that the affection you feel for one is actually felt for someone else? Do you imagine this manipulation to be gratifying?

But none of this is really the point is it, Vexed? Because meddling in the affairs of others is a great way to avoid looking into your own heart. Ask yourself why you are so concerned with the love lives of others and not of your own. Perhaps contemplating the idea of your own happiness makes you feel too unsettled, too confused. After all, to love someone is to give them power over you, to risk their displeasure. And you strike me as someone used to having all the power.

Much safer to distract yourself with telling others how to feel, for how can that hurt you? But one day you'll find someone you care about and you'll have to finally reckon with what it means to feel vulnerable. What will you do then? So, my dear, my advice is simple: leave the lives of your friends to them and instead engage in some self-reflection.

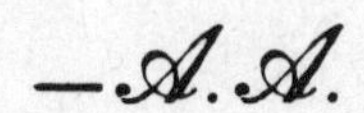

Dear Aunt Antigone:

My lover and I made a desperate, possibly ill-advised arrangement with someone very powerful. It seemed like the only way for us to be able to stay together. But it means I have to undertake a challenge that he has set for me. If I complete it, we'll be reunited. If I don't, I'll lose her forever. He called it a test of my faith in her.

I have no doubt whatsoever about her. He's *the one I don't trust. He's known for making hard bargains and playing dirty—he even kidnapped his own wife, and she's now forced to live with him for half the year. So what if this whole thing is a scam? What if he's lying? What if this test is just his way of having a laugh at my expense? Am I stupid for having trusted his word?*

Do I complete his challenge and hope for the best? Or am I being gullible and naive, letting him take advantage of me?

—Eyes Front

Dear Eyes:

Firstly, it's important to understand that your doubts are reasonable. Powerful forces are always trying to trick us, to offer us what we desperately desire, hoping that we don't see the catch until it's too late. I can't tell you if this is happening in your case, but I can help you through a little thought experiment.

For argument's sake, let's say that this test is real, that the deal is honest, and when you pass it, she'll be there for you. What is the cost of going through all that, of believing it's real? The distress you feel now, that uncertainty, that gnawing doubt—it's probably increasing with every moment that goes by, isn't it? It's probably consuming you.

Now, let's imagine that the distress and distrust are too great for you to tolerate and you don't complete his challenge . . . only to discover that the deal was fair. You will lose her forever, having traded your current temporary anguish for a more permanent misery.

On the other hand, what if you don't pass the test, and it turns out he was *lying to you? What are your options? Return and demand a new deal? Do you have that power? If you did, I'm guessing you wouldn't have found yourself in this position in the first place. You'd be just as lost. The same holds true for the scenario where he's lying and you complete his challenge. If you have no other leverage against this powerful manipulator, then there's nothing else you can do about it, is there? Both of these choices are irrelevant.*

You really have only two options where your choice matters: either you go all the way and get her back, or you give in to the fear and mistrust, and lose her. See, you're not really risking her at all. What you're actually up against is your own ability to tolerate feeling out of control. Yes, your fears are reasonable, but do you love her enough to sit with them, to push through them, to not give in to them? Can you live with the temporary uncertainty, with feeling this vulnerable?

If none of this helps, then try asking yourself this: Is your relationship with him more important than your relationship with her?

And while you're thinking about that, also ask yourself what choice she would make if she were in your position. How would she handle such a deal with the devil?

—A.A.

Dear Aunt Antigone:

I recently found out that the boy next door who I have loved for years was engaged to someone else, and I could not abide that. So I told him that he belonged with me, and we should run away together. And do you know what happened? He admitted that he cared for me but that he was going to marry that mealy-mouthed girl anyway! It was enough to make me see red!

That's not even the worst part—the whole thing happened where a rude and impertinent Charleston "gentleman" was eavesdropping. Afterward, he mocked me and called me "tempestuous." I told him that he was most definitely not a gentleman, and then he told me that I certainly wasn't a lady! It was mortifying!

But I am not one to accept these sorts of things without putting up a fight. I could try again to convince Ashley to marry me, and I know I would succeed. Or I could just marry that silly Charles Hamilton and drive Ashley mad with jealousy. I have a mind to do just that, except . . . would that prove Mr. Butler right in all the horrible things he said about me? What ever shall I do?

—Torn About Tomorrow

Dear Torn:

For starters, let's just sidestep the entire question of whether or not you can "make" anybody marry you, which is certainly a questionable endeavor no matter how desirable you believe yourself to be. And frankly, I have to wonder why you are only considering options that involve marriage. One boy, whom you regard as a possession, is engaged to a rival. The other is some poor boy whom you conveniently assume will fall at your feet. And what about this rival of yours? Is there something about her happiness that is so objectionable to you that you must thwart it?

You should also ask yourself why the Charleston man's words affected you so strongly. You describe it as "the worst part," but was he really that awful to you? Or might it be that, in spite of the show you put on for your targets, this man saw you for who you truly are, and you found the experience discomfiting?

And, Torn, why exactly do you need to be married? Does your life feel empty without another person? Is it a status marker in your world? Do you feel a void at the center of your soul, and are you driven to fill it with another person? Regrettably, more than a few marriages spring from that latter source. It may even provide a short-term sense of meaning and satisfaction. But eventually that will give way to resentment, because nobody can ever be strong enough, whole enough, perfect enough to be the rock on which you can build your own self.

If what you are really seeking is stability and a sense of meaning, then might I suggest what you need is not a husband, but a home? And that such a home can be found in many places other than marriage. Friendship, community, and social causes can give you a sense of belonging that won't require relying on a single person. However, even these concepts are a bit abstract. Perhaps what you are looking for is a physical manifestation of solidity that you can use to anchor yourself and that you can pour meaning into. An estate that is real. Love and land can both be cultivated, but only one can be held on to with your hands. And if you can build a home for yourself, you'll always have a place to go back to, no matter what tomorrow brings.

—*A.A.*

Dear Aunt Antigone:

I have some issues with the men in my life. First, I am engaged to a man whom I despise. I only agreed to the match out of obligation to help my father with his debts. There is a second man, of whom I'm fond, who has pursued my hand. He is very rich, and though he is a friend, I am not in love with him.

And there is one more. This man is a beast in many senses of the word. He is wild, untamed, and feral. He is also the most beautiful creature I have ever seen. A miracle that emerged from the last place anyone would expect—the deepest jungle. He makes me feel things I can't put into words.

My father and I, as well as our whole party, were marooned on an unnamed island, left to fend for ourselves. A horrible forest creature snatched me away, and I was convinced my life was at an end. And then he *appeared, like a forest god. He saved me. He kept me safe. Somehow, he could understand what I said, even though he could not speak English. I fell in love with him instantly.*

He brought me back to my father and disappeared into the forest. I promised I would wait for him always. But before he returned, we were rescued, and I left without him. I question that decision every day.

Back in the "civilized world," my ape-man seems like a dream. Were I free, I would go to him without hesitation. But I have obligations—I have made a promise of marriage, after all. I must honor my word.

How can I get my wild man out of my heart so I can do the thing I must do?

—Carried Away

Dear Carried:

Passion or duty? Reason or emotion? Honoring your word or honoring your feelings? This conflict is eternal.

I want to tell you to trust your heart. I want to tell you that you should throw caution and propriety to the winds and run away with your beast. He clearly is the one man who makes you feel alive. Surely that is a sign that you belong together. Were all things equal, there would be no contest.

Alas, you know that things are rarely, if ever, equal. You're making a difficult choice that will cause you pain, whatever you decide.

I am sorry to say that you will never get that wild man out of your heart. If you choose to not go with him, if you choose the "civilized" path of following through on your word and prioritizing familial obligation over your own happiness, then the pain of losing him will stay with you forever.

But pain fades. Pain can be tolerated. Humans are resilient creatures—we can adjust to pain or humiliation or isolation. We can find ways to survive in even the most challenging of environments. And you shall too, no matter if you choose to enter a loveless marriage out of obligation, or if you throw away convention and choose the one who makes you feels alive. Either way, you are strong enough to carry yourself through.

Dear Aunt Antigone:

She's perfect for me. She is the most beautiful woman in Wahlheim. She's selfless and giving, taking on the care of her siblings after her mother tragically died.

Even more, she too loves my favorite poet! She's the only other person who understands how heartbreakingly beautiful his work is. When I watch her reading it, her face lights up and her heart shines with divine fire. It's as if the heavens have ordained our meeting.

I cannot stop thinking about her. We are meant to be together. I am totally convinced of that. And I know she feels it too. If we can't be together, I don't know how I will go on.

So how can I prove to her that she should leave her husband and relieve my sorrows?

—Klopstock Lover

Dear Klopstock:

When a piece of art resonates with you—a poem, a song, a painting, anything—it feels as if it is a proxy for your essence. And when you find someone who appreciates that thing as much as you do, well, the headiness can be intoxicating. And thus, the work becomes a shorthand, a code that allows you to speak only to them, in your own secret language.

But the problem with speaking in code is that you can never be totally certain that what you are saying is exactly what is being heard.

The lifeblood of poetry is metaphor*—that is, poetry's essence lies in saying one thing is the same as another. But people are not metaphors. Relationships are not metaphors. Love is not a metaphor. This woman has an actual, nonmetaphorical marriage. If she wanted to end it and be with you, she would. Not doing that isn't a metaphor for anything; it's her choice.*

But do not despair. There are many other poetical constructions that can be just as powerful and enthralling as metaphor. For instance, you could spend some time with simile*—where one thing is described "as if it is like" another. Can you hear the difference, Klopstock? "Like" is not "same." Similar, maybe. Adjacent. "As if" is not "true," it's conditional, comparable.*

There is so much space in "as if." Enough space to breathe, to live.

Dear Aunt Antigone:

There's a boy. He's in my mind, my heart, my soul. He is more myself than I am. Sometimes I can't tell if we're actually two different people, or if we're two halves of the same spirit. We are creatures of the moors, and run off to spend our days there, alone, together. No one else understands. They all talk about love as if it were a business transaction, while we two are wild and free and pure. And yet . . .

On my recent visits to Thrushcross, I have gotten a glimpse of a different world. As much as the moors are in my blood, I find that the Grange excites a new, different ambition. I fear I will have to choose between my wild love and my dream for my own future.

Is there any way to have both?

—High on the Heath

Dear High:

Adults like to look at young people and make fun of them for how strongly and deeply they feel things. "It's like they think they're the first person to ever fall in love!" But as far as you know, you are the first person to ever feel the way you do.

Sometimes, the problem is words. When your body is filled with fire, ecstasy, trembling rage, or a bone-deep sense of connection with another, how can mere words accurately convey those feelings? It's tempting to reach for bigger metaphors, more intense adjectives, and rhetorical flights of fancy to try to convey just how much you're feeling.

But just as important as the words you use to describe this epic, world-shaking love, I wonder if you're also using these words to convey your feelings to the object of your affection. The problem with thinking you share a soul with someone is that you can forget to use your words. This may be hard to hear, dear, but you are not actually two parts of the same soul. You are two different people, with different minds, hearts, needs, and desires.

Now you've seen a new path, and so you're afraid he might not be able to walk with you. Are you sure he can't? Or does some part of you want him not to, want to keep this all for yourself? You say you have a wild love, and wildness can certainly be captivating. But love is also tender, nurturing, supporting. Is there room for that in your relationship?

Make sure you're telling him what's in your heart. Don't make him interpret signs or signals. Don't decide the limits of this great love, but instead give yourself a chance to discover them and maybe even push past them. Who knows, your love may surprise you with where he's able to follow you.

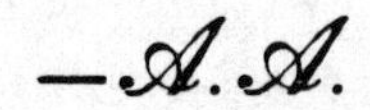

Chapter 2

NAVIGATING FRIENDSHIPS

Friendships can be as difficult and cumbersome to navigate as the deepest romantic relationships. Without constant attention, friendships too can wither and die, never to be resurrected. Misunderstandings left unspoken can fester until you discover your dearest friend has somehow become a mere acquaintance, or even worse, an enemy. Most of my friends were the sons and daughters of the ruling class in Thebes. They were my closest companions when times were good. When things turned bad, some of them abandoned me. I never forgot their betrayal; even centuries later, the recollection burns.

There may be fewer odes, songs, and epics written about friends, but that doesn't mean they're any less important than lovers or family. They can provide just as much strength, succor, and support, and they can cause just as much pain, suffering, and regret.

Dear Aunt Antigone:

I have a friend. He's obnoxious, rude, arrogant, puerile—truly a wretched little monster. But he's also, undeniably, a genius at what he does. Which is what we both do. And it's simply not fair!

I have spent years honing my compositions, learning how to play the game of attracting different patrons, sucking up to the right people. I did things the right way, paying my dues. I had great success. Or so I thought. Then he comes onto the scene in Salzburg, does everything wrong, breaks all the rules, gives offense to everyone important, and yet . . . he just sails from one triumph to the next.

The hardest part is that, I have to admit, the music he creates is so incredible, so visionary, that putting up with his awfulness is almost worth it. Almost. *But lately, I can feel myself curdling. I labor with every fiber of my soul to create something that isn't an abomination, and yet he can produce genius without even trying.*

If I have to endure his entitled, childish behavior much longer, I'm afraid I might kill him. I daydream about it. I find myself imaging plots, conspiracies, the elaborate methods I could use to do it.

I am not a violent man. I have music in my soul. I only wish to please God. There has to be another way I can learn to live with it, with him. *Isn't there?*

—Venomous in Vienna

Dear Venomous:

Friend *is such a flexible word, isn't it, that you can use it in regard to someone for whom you harbor so much antipathy? How does your "friend" feel about you, I wonder? I find that many people cultivate obnoxious, over-the-top personalities because they feel too vulnerable and scared to share their true feelings. Is there any chance your "friend" is one of them?*

Your agony is only made more acute by a healthy serving of cognitive dissonance. It appears that you live in a sphere where you are not permitted to, or are not comfortable enough to, express yourself freely. It is also possible that as much as you envy the work he creates, you also covet his ability to say what is on his mind and suffer no repercussions. You sound like a worldly person, seasoned, experienced, and not remotely a naïf. And yet, his behavior sends you straight into a child's refrain of "it's not fair!" It never fails to amaze me how easily we can be thrust right back to the injustices of our childhood.

I dearly hope that it does not need to be said, but to be certain, let me entreat you not to kill him. (Though I know that the odd murderous daydream is perfectly natural.) Instead, I'm going to challenge you to do something that you will find even more outrageous, and perhaps even more repugnant. You say he breaks rules and gives offense without consequence. But in my experience, consequences never disappear, they are only delayed. And the longer they are delayed, the more destructive they will eventually become. There will come a day when your "friend" will run out of triumphs and have nowhere to turn.

Knowing that this day is inevitable, you have a choice. You can choose to nurse your resentments, so that on that day you can join in what will undoubtedly be a festival of Schadenfreude *at your friend's expense. Or you can help him.*

I know that must feel counterintuitive to you, like the very last thing you wish to do. But consider this: What if you were the one person who didn't judge him? What if you could accept him for all of his egregious faults, even though they drive you mad? Would that feel like a lie to you? Perhaps at first. But the more you refrain from judging him, even when he deserves it, then the easier it will be for you to stop judging yourself so harshly.

Because the truth is that the venom and vitriol that you feel is ultimately not for your friend—it's for yourself. You are furious at yourself for not making music that you think is as great as his. But that is too much for you to feel, too great a burden to bear. Therefore, you displace your rage at a convenient target. That rage you feel? It is actually a poison, and until you get it out of your body, you will be its true victim.

But if you forgive him, support him, and act as his true friend instead of a counterfeit one, it is more likely that you will release the poison, and unlock gifts in yourself that you've never used before. And then who knows what wonders you might be able to create?

Dear Aunt Antigone:

My friend has a copious command of logic, among many other skills. It allows him to deduce things that I would never see on my own. I have lost count of the times he has declared some improbable thing to be true, and then gone on to show exactly how it came to be so. This impressive skill has helped him to not only build a thriving detective business, but also help countless innocents achieve justice and aid Scotland Yard in solving dozens of crimes that had been deemed "unsolvable." So, despite his unorthodox methods, I have always stood by him.

Except now, my friend has begun espousing something that I cannot in good conscience endorse. He has become convinced that the many disparate malevolent forces that beset us are all, in fact, working under the direction of one great criminal mastermind. I do not want to doubt my brilliant friend, especially in the face of so much previous evidence of his unparalleled perception, but his claim to such a monumental conspiracy defies all understanding. I am afraid that this mania could be the first sign of a nervous collapse brought about by overstimulation. But what if I'm wrong? It would not be the first occasion.

Is it sensible to believe that a single cause can explain so many different effects? Or is it merely an overactive mind imposing order where there is only chaos?

—Man of Inaction

Dear Inaction:

Reasons. We're all constantly looking for them. The more one invests in facts and logic, the more one thinks that there are reasons for everything. But even a cursory glance at the world will show that much of what happens is random, and that every effect has a million potential causes. When a mind gets used to making connections, finding those connections reliable, and getting rewarded for making those connections, it's only natural for that mind to think its power extends to everything.

A unified theory is so comforting, isn't it? It means everything has a place, and that the chaos in the world around us is merely some kind of intent in a framework we haven't worked out yet. So yes, it's entirely possible that your friend's behavior is the first sign of a nervous issue. However . . .

Crying "conspiracy" as a rhetorical device is certainly an overused tool on the part of the imprecise mind. But just because the word has been ill-used does not mean that the concept is wholly invalid. There have always been collusions of the powerful and various unspoken compacts. Relationships that take on a different character behind closed doors than they do in public. These kinds of conspiracies are all too real, common even.

Is it probable that behind all of these disparate forces there is a single person pulling the strings? Maybe not, but it's possible. Is it probable that your friend has gone too far? Perhaps, but maybe not. Do you have to decide either way right now?

Sometimes, a man of inaction is exactly what the situation calls for.

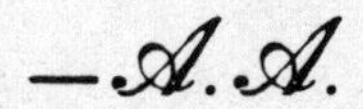

Dear Aunt Antigone:

H. has been my best friend for as long as I can remember. I never thought we'd let something as silly as boys *come between us. But somehow it happened, and I don't really understand why.*

One day, D. was telling me how much he loved me, and the next day he wouldn't even speak to me because he was so into her! She says she's only got eyes for L., but I know she's secretly enjoying all the attention. (I mean, I know I would.)

Anyway, it's turned into this whole thing. *It's too complicated to explain all of it, but let's just say she may have confided in me that she and L. were going to run away together—to the forest, of all places! So . . . I may have ratted her out to D. And now he's going to chase after them. I've got to chase after him too, right? I mean, what if he finds them and she changes her mind? What if something else happens? What if I miss it all?!*

I love her, I really do. She's been my best friend forever. But why does this all have to be so hard?

—Neglected Spaniel

Dear Spaniel:

It sounds like you've been through a lot already! Are you absolutely sure you want to follow them? Forests are dark, dangerous places, and you never know what mischief might be waiting for you.

As I see it, there are many different facets to this "whole thing," as you put it. But there's one central, crucial fact that should guide everything else that you do in this situation: you say that she is your best friend. You have had a long, close relationship, and maybe you thought on some level that it would always be the same. The advent of these boys, regardless of who likes whom—really, how are you keeping track?—means that the nature of your friendship has to change. It's understandable that you don't want that to happen, but it's inevitable. It would be difficult enough if you were dealing simply with drifting apart as you embarked on new romances. But now you stand to lose her completely.

So you spilled the details of her escape to a boy you say you want to love you—the same boy who threw you over for her. It's not too difficult to see that your interest here is not in either of these seemingly interchangeable suitors, but really in doing anything in your power to keep from losing your best friend. So now you've given yourself a reason to chase after her into the forest.

All change is hard, but this one is going to be especially dramatic. No matter what the outcome, your friendship will never be the same. If you can find a way to accept that, to honor what is was, and to relinquish it with love, you might find that the friendship will come back to you in new and surprising ways. For those who go into a forest are seldom the same when they come out of it.

Dear Aunt Antigone:

I have recently made the acquaintance of three men of great merit. Our initial introductions were somewhat antagonistic, which may have been my fault. I confess that I sometimes leap to conclusions or say the wrong thing at the wrong time, and it often lands me in hot water. In this case, I somehow found myself engaged in duels with all three of them on the same day. But when the cardinal's guards tried to arrest us, we banded together to fight them off. I saw them to be noble gentlemen, worthy of respect, honor, and friendship.

These men have much to teach me about swordplay, chivalry, and countless other topics, and I very much wish to learn. They are truly a noble trio that cannot be broken. But by virtue of their long service together and my only recent introduction, they have a great many jokes and allusions and meaningful glances among them that I simply do not understand.

So, I cannot help but feel like an outsider. And when I feel that way, I can easily lose my temper. I worry that I might then do or say something rash, and offend them all over again.

How can I make sure I won't alienate these new brothers? How can I make sure I fit in?

—*Fourth Wheel*

Dear Fourth Wheel:

Slow down there. Building a friendship is a process that takes time. Newly picked grapes cannot immediately become a robust and complex wine, no matter how much effort or desire they have. There is no substitute for allowing enough time for the process to unfold, in both wine and friendship. These men you admire have developed their camaraderie over years, through shared experiences. Their closeness is earned. The fact that your initial meetings were contentious and yet they still welcomed you into their circle, would seem to imply a generosity of spirit, or at least a healthy sense of humor. They are likely upstanding men.

You say that you get offended easily, which is often a sign of youth and insecurity. This trio has chosen not to hold that against you. This should tell you that you can relax around them. Easier said than done, certainly, but when they are laughing at some story or reliving some past exploit, that's the perfect time for you to ask them to tell you more about it. Most of us enjoy talking about ourselves, and the more you can be genuinely curious about them, the more they will open up to you.

And then before you know it, you'll have adventures together enough to develop your own shared bonds, and their trio may become a quartet.

Dear Aunt Antigone:

I moved to New York to take up the bond business, and I ended up renting a home out on Long Island, right on the shore of the Sound. My cousin lives across the bay with her husband, and through them I've made a new set of friends. They're rich, they throw amazing, extravagant parties almost every night, and we have a lot of fun. But also, if I'm being truthful, they're . . . awful. They're liars and cheaters and schemers. None of them tells the truth. They're all pretending to have a good time but really, they're all actually quite miserable, perpetually. And yet I can't bring myself to leave.

I like to think of myself as a straightforward, honest person. So why do I enjoy being around them so much?

—Egg Head

Dear Egg:

Why do we turn liars and scoundrels into heroes? Is it because most people are boring and normal, often confined by convention, and secretly wish they were free to do anything they wanted without fear of consequences? I'll bet that while you're among them you feel a little bit untouchable, like you're borrowing their glamour. Judging by how you speak of their wealth, it would be easy to get intoxicated, to do anything you can to impress them so you can stay in their orbit just a little bit longer.

There's another possibility. You say that you think of yourself as honest, but what if that's not true? What if you're just as dishonest as they are, and are simply hiding it from yourself? You certainly have no problem sitting in judgment of these so-called friends. Maybe you enjoy being with them because like calls to like, and you can indulge your own impulses to lie and cheat and scheme.

Or maybe it doesn't mean anything. Perhaps it's simply that they're rich, and rich people get away with all sorts of things. We all like to think that we're honest, good, upstanding people, but how many of us wouldn't trade that for freedom from consequences of our actions?

Perhaps you can spend some time trying to discern the difference between having a good time with awful people and having an awful time with good people. Can you differentiate between the two? How can you be sure?

Dear Aunt Antigone:

I have had a terrible falling-out with one of my closest friends. When I deigned to accept a proposal that she spurned, she behaved as if it were a personal affront. I love her dearly, but she can sometimes be quite full of herself. She can be contemptuous when others do not meet her high standards and is easily prejudiced by first impressions. My new husband clearly falls short in her eyes.

My friend and I continue to correspond as much as we ever did, but I can tell that things are different. Her letters are quite removed, more formal than they ever were before. It grieves me, but I do not regret my choice to marry, however much she wishes to judge me. I will admit that my husband is neither sensible nor agreeable. But at the age of twenty-seven, I was well aware that my choices were between him and living the remainder of my life as an old maid.

I am not romantic. I never was. This was the best chance I would ever have for my establishment. But I miss my friend and the close companionship we once had. Will it ever return? Or have I lost her forever?

—Unapologetic Collins

Dear Unapologetic:

It seems like a lot has happened in your life recently, and because of that, your friendship can never go back to the way it was before. But give your friend more time to adjust to your new reality. With luck she will come to appreciate that, high standards or not, you have your own values and needs.

In some respects, no matter the nature of the first impressions or opinions of the match's agreeability, this sort of shift is inevitable whenever one friend marries and another does not. Your whole life is now shared with another person, and your friend is not invited. The entire calculus is shifted. Even in the most harmonious situation, there is bound to be a certain amount of friction, even resentment at first. And this appears to be far from harmonious. Especially since, as it seems, your friend is not in a relationship of her own. There is now a sudden empty place in her life, and she likely does not know how to fill it.

You are right to point out to her that she is acting out of turn, while at the same time you can also choose to read her behavior as an expression of her care for you. She only wants the best for her friend, and if her assessment of what that is does not match with your own, then ultimately, it's up to her to respect your decision.

You have, in some respect, forged ahead of her into an area of knowledge that she is ignorant of—married life. One day, perhaps, she will follow you, and the experience may teach her some things that will change her estimation of your own choices. I suggest that you give her some time and perhaps she'll eventually open back up to you. If she doesn't, then you'll know she values her prejudices above your friendship. But if she does, you would be well within your rights to expect an apology.

I suggest that you think about how that conversation might go, and what you would require from it. In some ways, you will need to treat her like another kind of suitor. And where your husband's proposal appealed to your reason, any suit from your friend will have to satisfy your heart.

—A.A.

Dear Aunt Antigone:

My best friend is everything I aspire to be—unworried, unhurried, and free. He's also generous and he's shared so much of his rich life with me. He's made me feel for the first time that I belonged somewhere. I came to Italy on a mission to persuade him to come home, but now I never want to leave.

But something has happened, and I'm not sure what. Lately, he's been pushing me away, withdrawing, and I don't like it. I told him I was sorry for whatever it was I did, but he keeps saying everything is fine. I don't believe him. I know he's angry with me. It might be because he caught me trying on some of his clothes. It was completely harmless, though. I told him that, and I thought he believed me. More likely, it's his awful girlfriend. She hates me, but only because she knows that she doesn't deserve him. I think she's poisoning him against me. I can see it in the way he looks at me now.

We'd been talking for a while about a trip to Paris, but now he's suddenly uninterested. I did convince him to take a shorter trip with me. Only three nights. But there's a feeling of awful finality about it. It feels like the last chance to fix things between us. But how? I'm willing to do anything, take the most drastic action, if it will keep us together.

—Imposter Syndrome

Dear Imposter:

Friendships have an ebb and a flow to them. They can start out as hot and heavy as any romance, only to cool when people grow more comfortable with each other. You may not believe this in the midst of your current distress, but this is actually a good sign, as it signals a transition to something that can be more mature, adult, and honest.

When it reaches that point, you don't have to be perfect around each other. To some extent, we begin all relationships as performers, playing a version of our self that we hope the other will respond to. But nobody can do that indefinitely. It's exhausting. Eventually you just have to be you.

Right now, you're sensing that your friend is closing himself off. Judging from your desperate tone, I'll guess that you're tempted to enlarge your performance, to do more, to be more of the person you were when he first met you. But that will only exacerbate the situation, unbalancing the dynamic between you two further. The path to an even keel is to loosen your grip, to be more of your true self and less of the person you think he wants you to be.

Even then, you can't make him—or anybody for that matter—stay in your life. All you can do is be who you are and hope that he will accept the real you, imperfections and all.

Dear Aunt Antigone:

The world is a dangerous place. I didn't know that when I was younger, and some bad things happened. Daddy said I had to be punished. So now I don't go out much and never during the daytime. Only at night. It's a lot safer to stay inside. Everybody says so.

I haven't really talked to anybody besides my family in a while. But lately, I've been wondering if I should try. There are some children who live near me. A brother and sister, and their friend. They remind me a lot of how I used to be. Exploring, curious, getting into things that they shouldn't.

I don't think they know just how dangerous the world can be, even in a little Alabama town like ours. I think I want to help them. I think it might be nice to have some new friends. But I'm not really sure how to do that anymore. And I'm worried that they might be scared of me.

What should I do?

—Friendly Ghost

Dear Ghost:

I get the impression that you are in a vulnerable place. And even from the little that you describe, I'm not entirely sure that staying inside your home so much is as safe as you think. Perhaps these "bad things" you mention continue to haunt you. But who is in there with you? Do they truly have your best interests at heart? I know that it's not what you've written in to ask about, but I can't help but feel that it's connected.

Making friends isn't easy for a lot of people. Gone are the days when you could just walk up to someone you didn't know and start talking to them. Nowadays, we're all guarded and watchful, full of opinions and stories about each other. It can be hard to see who's really in front of you, even when they're looking you right in the eye. You've got a story you're telling yourself about these neighborhood children: they're innocent, naive, and unprepared for the harsh truths of the world. But you don't really know that, do you? Maybe it's true. Maybe they're going to have to learn about the dangers for themselves. After all, everyone does, sooner or later.

Children can be cruel and quick to judge. You, Ghost, sound like you need friends who are going to be gentle with you, as you learn how to interact and become comfortable with them. If you do try to befriend your neighbors, do yourself (and them) a favor and go slowly. Don't come on too quickly or strongly. Expect some misunderstandings and try not to get easily frustrated. Perhaps you can break the ice with some small act of service or generosity? Just a little thing would likely do. I believe that they may be as skittish as you.

Dear Aunt Antigone:

I simply know too much. My head is full of facts and histories, insights and connections, past tragedies and future calamities. It can be a heavy burden. So to help ease that load, I like to spend time with friends. Two in particular: a dear former traveling companion from an old adventure and his nephew, a sweet, openhearted boy. They come from a village full of small, earthy folks who live in fastidious little "holes." Whenever I visit, I bring fireworks, enjoy their excellent pipe-weed, and amuse myself at their antics. So far away from the great troubles of the world, it is peaceful and I am rejuvenated.

But those troubles are growing manifestly closer, and soon there will be no place to hide from them. And so, my friend's nephew is about to undertake a dangerous journey at my behest. I've told him of some of the dangers he might face, but I have held back crucial information. If he knew the whole truth, he might choose not to go. But he must. So much depends on it. Part of me wishes to tell him everything and let him make a fully informed choice. But a larger part of me is convinced that the knowledge would be too much for him to take in.

If I don't tell him everything, and he walks into his doom unaware, will I ever be able to forgive myself?

—Grey Area

Dear Grey Area:

How pleasant it must be for all those people not like you and me, walking around free of a head crammed full of knowledge. And how nice that you've managed to find simple folk who can help you feel better about your burdens.

But you and I both know that people like that can't really be trusted to make their own choices, can they? Without the vast stores of insight that you possess, how could they? And it puts you in an awkward position, either overwhelming them with a flood of information that they can barely keep up with, or else laboriously trickling it out drop by drop so they don't drown in it.

I don't suppose your young friend, with his little mind, could be trusted to make sense of everything you know and make the right decision—that is, the decision you want him to make. It is so much easier to tell him just what will induce him to do things your way. After all, you know better, don't you?

Or maybe, just maybe, if he knew everything you did, your little friend might surprise you. How will you ever find out if you don't give him the chance? He may be wiser than you think.

Chapter 3

RECEIVING *an* EDUCATION

When I was young, girls were simply not sent to school. While my brothers were sent off to study history, philosophy, geometry, warcraft, and other scholarly topics, I stayed home and learned "domestic" arts from my mother. I spent hours learning how to weave and sew, and studying all the ways to run a household. When my brothers left in the mornings for school, I would pine to go with them. When they came home, I'd pester them to tell me everything they could remember from their day's lessons and soak up everything I could. I would fantasize about being allowed to go with them to their school, of meeting other students and forming lifelong friendships and bonds, of testing myself and my intellect in Socratic discussions and debates, of winning public competitions through my skill at oration and athletics, my mastery of philosophy and rhetoric. In my imagination, the school was a temple, a place of high aspiration and noble purpose.

Later, I would learn the truth—no matter how perfect the aims of education, it is still the province of fallible people. Often, the most indelible teachings are not part of the official curriculum, for better or for worse. School is the place where the idyllic fantasies and naive projections of youth crash into the cold realities of the world. Many of those lessons are hard, and they can last a lifetime.

Dear Aunt Antigone:

Three weeks ago, I went to the school for the first time. There are a lot of nice girls in school and we had scrumptious fun playing. The schoolmaster, he didn't like me right away. He called my spelling dreadful and teased me for being so far behind the others. But it was splendid anyway. Then that boy showed up. Everyone says he's so handsome, and I suppose he is, but he's also a troublemaker. He teases the girls so horribly.

I resolved to not let his teasing affect me whatsoever. But I would never have guessed how awful he could be when he made fun of the color of my hair in front of everyone. So I cracked my slate over his head. He deserved it! But did he get in trouble for saying such horrid things to me? No! The schoolmaster blamed me! He said I had a vindictive spirit!! Can you imagine?!

My feelings were hurt excruciatingly. But I resolved to go on. Only, the next day, when everybody was late getting back from dinner, I was the only one who got punished for it! Mr. Phillips hates me so much that he made me sit next to the new boy for the whole rest of the day. It was mortifying!

Obviously, I can never show my face in that schoolhouse ever again. Everyone else tells me that it's not so bad and that I should just forget it and go back. How can I make them understand that I really have been humiliated in a way that I will carry with me forever?

—Cordelia in Exile

Dear Cordelia:

While I do not know the specific truancy laws in your community, when children stop showing up at their school it tends to cause issues. So while I applaud your resolve, I would advise that you prepare yourself for the eventuality of returning.

When you do, you will hear a lot of advice from friends and loved ones. They will try to convince you that your feelings of humiliation are overblown. That what you suffered was not that bad. That everyone in school has to deal with moments where they are punished unfairly or have to submit themselves to a teacher who does not have their best interests at heart, or who catches unwanted attentions from a classmate. They will tell you to stop being so sensitive.

Don't listen to them.

Oh, it may mean that you have to suffer additional humiliations and terrible injustices. It may mean that when you are subjected to the same pains and pressures as everyone else that you will feel them more keenly, more intensely than others. You may be tempted to try to outgrow those feelings. My dear, resist.

You're right when you say that you will carry these humiliations with you forever. Given time, they will sink out of your memory, but they will still be in there somewhere. You can't make events that happened not have happened. But you can control what happens next.

If and when you return, they will try to get you to admit that you overreacted and that your emotions must come second to the needs of the school. Tell them whatever they want to hear, but don't let them convince you they're right. Because if you do, you may start to believe that you cannot trust your first reactions to whatever the world sends your way. Many people learn to distrust their own feelings and bury them in the face of more "reasonable" attitudes from others. Better if you can stay true to yourself, regardless of how much others think you overly emotional, intense, wrong, or inappropriate.

The real challenge isn't how to convince others to believe your feelings; it's how to ensure you don't lose that belief in those feelings. Because if that happens, you'll find yourself in exile no matter where you are.

Dear Aunt Antigone:

I am a student of the sciences and natural philosophy at the University of Ingolstadt. Throughout my tenure there, the professors have given me nothing but high praise. For a time, I thought I might be capable of great feats, or monumental discoveries that would change the world. I wanted to accomplish something no one else had done before. Not too long ago, I thought I was on the verge of such a discovery. I thought I had uncovered the secret of life, of how to create it where none existed. I imagined a new world, one where death was banished, where no one need feel loss, where I would be revered as a Titan. I worked myself into a frenzy trying to achieve this miracle that I was convinced was possible.

And then I did it. But when I witnessed the results of my experiment, I realized how misguided I had been. I was stricken with horror and remorse, and thus I buried all evidence of what I had done. Shortly thereafter, I fell ill, whether from overwork or shock, and it was months before I could regain the strength to return to school. But since my experiment, everything has been different.

Where once I lived for the approval and regard of my professors, now whenever they compliment my work or my ideas, I am filled with revulsion. This place of learning, which once I thought would become the cradle of my great ambitions, is now a prison. I feel watched, hunted even, by a malevolence that trails me night and day. I dream about quitting and going home to Geneva, to marry, start a family, and put all thought of scientific achievement behind me, but I fear that I will never be able to escape the monstrosity of what I've done. My best friend perpetually tries to dissuade me from withdrawing. He wants me to join him in the study of foreign languages. Perhaps that would be enjoyable. But to be truthful, the prospect only fills me with exhaustion. I'm not sure I should even bother.

Do I abandon school and flee the specter of my greatest failure? Or do I stay, try to forget it ever happened, and recommit myself to my education?

—Frankly Defeated

Dear Frankly:

You could certainly choose to go home. But your "failure," as you call it, will follow you, no matter where you go. It's always in your mind, so there's no way for you to outrun it.

After such an unsettling experience, it's clear that you're trying to use sober calculation and rationality to decide on a new path. But, Frankly, I have to tell you that underneath your science and your philosophy, you do not sound to me like someone who makes momentous choices without becoming seized by passion and fire.

But let us, for a moment, indulge your pretense of sober deliberation. You could listen to your friend, choose to stay at university, and pursue a different course of study. But in such proximity to your old haunts, the site of so much toil and ambition, could you resist relapsing into your old habits? To stay in arm's reach of your former glory without touching it, would it drive you mad? Or would you find yourself drifting back to the scene of the crime, like a drunk seeking just one more sip of wine? If this is true, then why bother hiding from it in the first place? Do not try to pretend to be something you are not. If you are a natural scientist, then be a natural scientist!

Oh, but then there's the matter of your great failure, to which I say, "so what?" Is not a university exactly the sort of place where one is expected to try and fail and try again? How else are you supposed to learn if you are not permitted to make mistakes?

Of course, maybe it's not the failure itself that causes you so much pain. Maybe it's how the experience of this failure has colored the way others see you, or more likely, the way you see yourself. Perhaps it showed you things about yourself that you didn't know were true. You would not be the first to arrive at university believing that you were one type of person, only to leave with the knowledge that you are actually somebody else. This is sometimes called "character-revealing." Mistakes, failures, disasters, and other such calamities are all character-revealing events. They can inspire you to learn hidden truths about yourself, or they can push you to flee from the knowledge that you are unwilling to accept. Which is it for you?

What if, instead of hiding from your failure, you were able to embrace it? What might you see then? What might you learn, about yourself, about the world, about life?

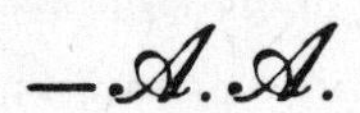

Dear Aunt Antigone:

I got expelled from school today. I just can't bring myself to try anymore. It's all just so pointless. Why does everybody care about this garbage? I don't really care, it's all full of phonies anyway. Cheesy. I don't even know why I'm writing to you. You're probably a phony too.

I'm not being overly dramatic, but I'm seriously asking—what's the point? In anything? Why bother trying if it's all going to turn to crap anyway?

—Buck Hat

Dear Buck:

One of the hardest things about growing up is the moment when you first understand how much you've been lied to for your whole life.

As children, we are all amateur scientists. We study the world around us, attempting to influence it, watching how it responds, and adjusting our understanding. When we're young, we want to know everything. We believe everything we're told—for how can we not? And when we're young, our parents are gods. They can answer any question, solve any problem.

Trouble begins the moment we notice that our parents are not infallible. That their knowledge is imperfect. At first, we make excuses for them. We tell ourselves stories. We convince ourselves that it's our *fault, that we need something more—age, experience, wisdom—and then we will surely see things just as our parents do.*

But as time goes on, the truth becomes undeniable. The gods are fallible. The rules aren't real. What we thought was bedrock is just smoke. Everything that was wonderful turns to ashes.

I know that you won't appreciate me telling you that everyone goes through this. When consumed by such isolating despair, nothing is worse than some stranger telling you that your feelings are cheap, common. Perhaps this might be a little more palatable: the ones who have the hardest time are the ones who believed the most. Meaninglessness only matters if you cared desperately for meaning in the first place. Without it, everything is pointless, phony, cheesy.

I love that you used the word cheesy. *It tells me everything I need to know about you. Something is "cheesy" when it's built on a consensual lie. Everyone pretends that the cheesy thing has value; it's great, exciting, delicious, oozing with creamy, fatty satisfaction. But that satisfaction is a mirage masking a twofold emptiness—from not being nourished and from knowing that you're participating in the lie. But you have chosen, defiantly, to no longer participate in that lie. I imagine you loudly proclaiming that lie wherever you find it, making sure to keep yourself apart from all the liars. Pointing the finger at them and naming them for what they are. But that can't change the fact that you're still starving for something to believe in, for some new meaning to jam into the empty space created by your disillusionment.*

I'm going to be honest with you, Buck. This is a very dangerous time for you. You present a strong, principled front and an air of detachment. Underneath, though you may not know it, you're yearning for something, anything, *to believe in. I'll bet that you're practically radiating with that need.*

It will make you a target.

All kinds of people, forces, ideologies, philosophies, movements, and cabals will be eager to sell themselves to you, for you are their favorite kind of mark—smart, perceptive, suffering, and desperate for anything to make the pain go away.

You've been abandoned by the gods, which I know is terrible. But it also sets you free. Now, you get to choose what you want to believe in. I can't tell you what that should be. Just try to make it something that nourishes your own soul without harming anyone else's.

Dear Aunt Antigone:

For my whole life, I have loved reading, studying, learning. But in Wessex, these activities are looked at with suspicion, even hostility. There was no one who could teach me, so I did my best to educate myself. I dreamed of one day being accepted to study at Christminster University, even though everyone told me I was crazy, that a common drudge like me didn't belong there. They mocked me and teased me and told me to give up my dream. And I did, a few times. Life isn't easy.

But eventually, I did it. I left my home and moved near the university. I took a job with a stonemason to support myself, and I keep up my own studies when I can. But nobody from the school will even reply to my entreaties. I can't even qualify for one of the few scholarships available to the poor. The students whom I've met are lazy and foolish—I know more than they do, but it's still not enough for me to be accepted.

Nobody cares that a stonemason from a nowhere village burns to become a scholar. But I keep hanging around, hoping to find some way to get them to accept me. Am I being foolish? Were all of them right to tell me to give up this dream? Should I quit, go home, and accept my place among the poor obscure people?

—Outsider at the Gates

Dear Outsider:

I heartily empathize with your struggle. It can be heartbreaking to feel like you have a calling when the world continually tells you that you're wrong.

But I have a secret to tell you, Outsider. The world does that to everyone. I don't say that to devalue what you are going through—not at all. Anybody who makes a choice to pursue a particular road or path will find themselves beset by obstacles, by malevolent forces trying to stop them. This is because your desire makes you notice all the things that stand in your way.

I'll bet you go through your day making a million decisions that don't trouble you at all—because you don't care much about them. Some would call this irony: "Why are the things that don't matter so easy, while the important things are impossible?" But the very act of designating something as important, the act of caring about it, the act of wanting it, makes the pain of failure so much keener that we become highly attuned to it, and notice it first.

Some people approach this problem by adopting an attitude of not wanting anything at all. Of disclaiming their goals, of pretending they are perfectly fine with whatever comes their way. If you give up your dream, perhaps you will find yourself on this path, trying to convince yourself that you never really wanted it in the first place. Many people need to do this to survive and to hold on to their sanity. But I would counsel you to look in a different direction.

There's something else you're yearning for in addition to that scholarly life. You are also yearning for acceptance. *That is, you want what you want, and you want it to be permissible to want what you want. These are two entirely different things.*

One is under your control—nobody can stop you from reading whatever you want, from learning whatever interests you, from letting your curiosities lead you down whichever roads you choose. The other is not—you cannot control how other people value you. You cannot force anyone to accept you; you can only try to surround yourself with people who do. It sounds like you haven't had many places of acceptance over the course of your life. So maybe this university will never accept you. Have you considered that if they cannot see your value, then you are better off without them?

Your challenge is not how to convince them to let you inside the gates. It's to find a way to accept yourself, even if they never do. To give yourself permission to want what you want, and not need anyone's approbation to tell you that you are pursuing the proper path.

I don't mean to suggest this is easy. But it can be done, and you don't need anyone else's permission to do it.

Dear Aunt Antigone:

Ma and Pa decided it was finally time that I go to school. My sister Mary and I walked into the town, and I was very excited. When we got there, some of the boys started calling us names and making fun of us, but some of the other children were nice.

But there's one girl at the school who is not nice at all. Her name is Nellie Oleson and she's just about the meanest person I've ever seen! When she first saw us, she called us "country girls"! Mary said it was true, since we really are country girls, but Nellie meant it to be mean. She just thinks she's better than everybody else!

I want to do well in school and make the teacher proud of me. But Nellie makes me so mad that sometimes I can't think of anything else except getting back at her. I could slap her, if only Pa wouldn't get mad at me.

How can I get her to stop wrinkling her nose at me?

—Pint Full of Sore

Dear Pint Full:

I understand your frustrations. School is supposed to be for learning. But there are other types of learning besides reading, writing, and 'rithmetic. One of the most important things we can learn by going to school is how to interact with all kinds of different people and meet children from many different backgrounds. These classmates of ours may come from different cultures, ethnicities, or countries. They may speak different languages and even have ways of acting and talking that seem strange at first.

On the other hand, oftentimes at school, you'll even meet someone who seems like they should be very similar to you, like they come from the same kind of place, but they behave in a totally different way. This Nellie sounds like one of those people.

I know you're angry with her now, and it sounds like that anger is justified. But was there a moment before you decided that you were angry? Can you remember when that was, what you felt like then? Can you remember what you thought when you saw this Nellie for the very first time? You may not want to remember it now, but I'll bet you were excited. I bet you thought that she was someone that you might be able to make a friend with.

Now, you don't have to be friends with everybody—that would be asking too much of anyone. I am simply wondering if the anger you feel is so large because on some level you are disappointed. It's perfectly fine if you feel that way.

I just want you to remember that the people we are in school are not always the people we become later in life, and that it's all right if you hold on to some small hope that perhaps one day she will see you differently enough to become your friend.

In the meantime, listen to your pa and do not slap her.

Dear Aunt Antigone:

I was fortunate enough to study under a great professor of metaphysico-theologo-cosmolo-nigology. While the education I have received from him has been wide and various, it is all connected by a single central thread, which he called "optimism." In his view, everything that happens in the world—no matter how bad, or painful, or destructive—is for the best. He contends that there is no version of the world that can be better than the one we are in, because it is the only one that exists.

I am nobody of rank or importance, so far be it from me to question such an illustrious philosopher. Yet, when I look at the world, I confess that I see a great many things that belie his teachings. Especially as of late. Not too long ago, the baron threw me out of my home, merely for falling in love with his daughter, Cunégonde. Furthermore, I was conscripted into an army and forced to fight in several horrible battles.

I eventually escaped and made my way to Belgium, where I found the great professor again. He had become a beggar after the baron, Cunégonde, and their entire family had been killed in an attack. And yet, he still professed his belief that this world is the best one possible.

I don't wish to sound ungrateful, but I do confess that when I tell myself that all is well . . . I'm not sure I believe myself anymore.

What do you think—do we actually live in the best of all possible worlds? Or might the great professor be in error?

—Cautiously Optimistic

Dear Cautiously:

There are a lot of names for the idea that your great professor preaches: Optimism, Providence, God's Mercy, the Will of the Universe. It's attractive, isn't it?

Everyone loves an optimist. It's so heartening to see someone who, beset by life's troubles, can look past them and find a reason to keep going, to keep a smile on their face. Optimism is powerful, and I don't mean to suggest it's not.

However, there's a trick to optimism. It has to be self-generated, self-discovered, wholly chosen. If you can find your own well of optimism, then you have a bedrock on which to build a life that can weather even the most terrible of storms.

The error your professor is guilty of is failing to see that optimism cannot be taught. It cannot be prescribed. Providence is a poor answer to an actual problem, like describing a loaf of bread to a person who is starving. The idea does not sate the hunger.

What's worse is that relentless optimism can quickly become a cudgel. In subscribing to this ideology, it would hold then that if optimism is the solution to all your problems, then any problems you have must result from you not being optimistic enough. It's your fault. So you shouldn't stand up and ask for, or demand, the things you need. Don't ask to be fed, sheltered, cared for, respected, or loved. Instead, just try harder to think the right way. Needless to say, this simply isn't feasible, dearie. Alas, too many are caught up in this fallacy.

Genuine optimism cannot be felt by choosing to ignore the real problems in front of your face. It can only be reached by looking squarely at them, taking action to counteract as much as possible, and finding a way to be content with the outcome. That *is the best of all possible worlds.*

—*A.A.*

Dear Aunt Antigone:

I'm the first person in my family to go to college, and my family sacrificed a lot to send me here—more than you can imagine. But it didn't take me long to realize that I don't belong here, not at all. Here in the North, everything is so strange. They are not burdened by their past, not haunted by time. No, Harvard is no place for someone like me, it's so painfully clear, and yet my family's honor demands that I endure, no matter how much pain it causes me. Not that anyone else in the family much cares for honor.

My roommate, a Canadian of all things, is a nice enough fellow, even if he keeps stealing my trousers. My classes and my professors and my fellow students spend all of their time studying about and talking about and debating about the past but thinking about talking about dreaming about their futures. Mostly, I just dream about my sister and the shame of it all.

I just can't escape the feeling that something is irretrievably wrong inside of me, and that I carry it with me wherever I go. I don't belong here, and I don't belong at home in Jefferson. I don't belong in the present or the past. The future signifies nothing. So where else can I go?

—Drowning In Honeysuckle

Dear Drowning:

Some people spend their entire lives in the vicinity of the same few dozen people. The same faces, the same stories, the same parties, forever. Those people know more about someone in their community who died long ago than they do about someone living just on the other side of the mountain or lake or some other uncrossable social divide. Some are content with this; others don't have an option. But most, especially the young, have a low tolerance for this boredom. They push to strike out, to find new places, new stories, and new communities. They travel, move to different lands, join armies, or, like you, go off to college. They look for places where people live differently, know different stories, and have different ways of looking at the world.

Perhaps this isn't you. Perhaps you are only at your school because of family pressure, and if left to your own devices, you would have stayed home. But you say that you don't belong at home. Might there be something to that whiff of shame surrounding your sister? You don't say, but let's assume that on some level, you wanted to get away.

Now you've gotten what you wanted. A whole world of different kinds of people, who think differently, act differently, tell different stories about themselves, and make their own decisions about what they think about you without knowing all the history and background and stories that the people you grew up around would know.

Some people find this intoxicating. They invent totally new identities for themselves, and they never look back. Others have trouble negotiating this transition but emerge on the far side to find that they are still themselves, only with a few new chosen habits and outlooks that they've picked up from colliding with others.

But some simply cannot make the leap. Like you, they can't let go of where they came from enough to latch on to something new. Instead, they hover in the middle, unanchored.

If there really is something wrong inside of you, now is the perfect time to pull it out, examine it, and decide if you want to keep it or not. Because despite what you may have learned, you can make that decision. You can allow yourself the space to grow, to evolve.

So, go steal a Canadian's pants, or skip a class, or give away your watch. Anything you can think of, or something you can't think of. Just because your past contains no known instances of similar behavior doesn't mean that your right-now can't.

We may never fully escape our past, but we can loosen our grip on it, the grip it has on us, and allow ourselves to live more fully in the present. If you can do that, the future will take care of itself.

Dear Aunt Antigone:

I study sculpture at the Rhode Island School of Design. A series of strange and unsettling occurrences has happened to me and several of my classmates recently, and I'm not sure what to do about them.

I've always been what my family has described as "sensitive." And I know that behind my back, others called me worse things: "neurotic" and "queer."

Clay is my preferred medium, and I often use it to create what I see in my dreams. Those unconscious visions guide my hands, and often I have no understanding of the shapes that they create. Hideous gaping jaws, snakes with grasping tentacles, dripping with green ooze. Unfathomable landscapes, great cyclopean monoliths, every night a new horror invades my dreams. Lately, these visions have grown clearer, as if they are becoming more real, and I can see the full breadth of a great and sinister city, malice and doom radiating from every structure. Hieroglyphics of an indecipherable language cover every surface, and these same symbols have begun showing up carved into the surfaces of my sculptures. Uncanny, unnerving, and unsettling, it is!

For a long time, I kept this to myself, for I thought I was the only one suffering these spells. However, I've come to discover that I am not alone, and that many of my other classmates are having similar nightmares. These horrors are only growing stronger, and with them comes a mounting sense of foreboding, as if a terrible, eldritch slumbering thing is rumbling toward a wakefulness we will all regret. All attempts to communicate this to the college's faculty, administration, and responsible parties have been met with only derision and denial. Growing despair and a sense of futility grip me and my classmates. Nobody in authority is going to save us from this eldritch doom, so how do we save ourselves?

—Indelibly Accursed

Dear Accursed:

Pity the close-minded. Help them see if you can, but some people will never accept anything they can't physically hold in their hands. "Nothing that is not logical is real," they'll contend. Graciously remove yourself from that conversation. Live long enough, and it becomes clear that this world is filled with the illogical, irrational, and inexplicable. Understanding that logic has its limit is the first step toward wisdom. If your "authorities" do not know that, then how much authority do they really carry?

Might these visions really be coming from you? Grown in some deep well of sinister imagination and invention? Let out through your sculptures and unconsciously picked up on by your fellow students? We are more susceptible to contagious ideas than most people think. None of us really know where our dreams come from—perhaps we transmit them to each other like psychic broadcasts. And if that was true, we could easily explain away your visions as made-up, unreal, mental noise. Faulty signals, nonsense on which we try to impose meaning. However, you don't believe that, and neither do I.

Cruel fate has decided that you can see the world differently. To you is given knowledge and insight. How I wish you had been spared this burden. Ultimately, you will find that most of the world will punish you for your ability to see. Let that roll off your back if you can. Hoping for help from authorities who will not take your fear seriously is a waste of your time. Understand that if something horrible truly is coming, then the only way you will withstand it is by finding others who see the danger too.

Right now, you and your classmates need to accept that you can only rely on yourselves. Let everyone else go—if they will not stand with you, then get them out of your way. You need to find as many like-minded folks as you can. Especially the ones who can see the truth but cannot yet allow themselves to believe it. Help them to overcome their doubts, and they can become your firmest allies.

We humans, as a species, are never prepared for the rules of our world to totally change. Getting people to act against a danger they cannot see is almost impossible. Artists like you are usually at the forefront of pivotal moments like this. Historically, it's the sensitive people like us who are called on to lead others from ignorance into insight. Now you must decide if you are up to the moment. And if you are, then your task is clear. Get your sculptures seen by as many people as possible. Let your visions be seen by as many eyes as possible.

Find the others, for there are like-minded souls out there who are ready to see what you see. Help them understand, if you can. Tell your story, even in the face of ridicule and contempt. A lonely individual beset by visions of a looming apocalypse is considered mad. Gather enough comrades, though, and you can turn madness into meaning, transforming your visions into a map, a blueprint for preparing for whatever monsters loom on the horizon. No other course can lead you through oncoming darkness to whatever light shines on the other side.

Chapter 4

BODY, MIND, and SPIRIT

Toward the end of his life, I cared for my father. At that point, he was blind and overwhelmed by depression. I have since wondered if sacrificing his own sight led to his despair, or was it the other way around? These causes and effects can be impossible to disentangle. But we have to start somewhere.

Illness is a fact of life. How we react to it shapes our experiences; we can be at its mercy, try to ignore it, or accept it as a fact and endure the best we can. At one point or another, everybody faces this. If you haven't yet, just wait.

Even under the best of circumstances, life challenges us all. Add in a disease, disability, or a physical or mental illness, and those challenges increase exponentially. This struggle is difficult enough on its own. It gets immeasurably harder when the world labels a suffering person as an "other."

We don't, as a society, handle illness well. We want to define everything as a discrete set of symptoms, behaviors, problems . . . so we can find a simple, effective solution that allows everything to return to normal as quickly as possible. But too often, physical and mental conditions are so intertwined that they cannot be easily separated, cataloged, or cured. And as for "normal," who gets to define what that is? I get many letters from readers dealing with these kinds of struggles, and no matter the myriad differences in their stories, the one thing they all have in common is the grief of being outside of that definition.

Dear Aunt Antigone:

On a recent morning, I discovered upon waking that I had come down with a certain condition. I hesitate to go into too much detail about the specifics of this condition, but let us say that I felt quite transformed from myself. I have no idea how this happened, and to be honest, I haven't really spent a whole lot of time thinking about it. Things happen in this world, don't they? And we must endure them for the sake of others.

I, for, instance, am a traveling salesman. It is not a job that I like, but I am working to pay off my parents' debts. I have been at this firm for fifteen years, and I think in about five or six more I will have enough to pay everything off. (If I didn't have my parents to think about, I would give my notice this very day.)

Anyway, that morning, I woke up late, having slept through my alarm. That's never happened before. I am up at 4:00 a.m. every day to get to work on time and I've never been late. Such uncharacteristic behavior was sure to get me in trouble with the boss, so I immediately tried to get out of bed and rush to work as quickly as possible. I thought perhaps I could get the 7:00 a.m. train. But I quickly discovered that my condition made that quite challenging. All the noise and commotion attracted the notice of my parents and my poor sister. I tried to keep them from seeing me in my altered state, but when they finally did, it caused so much upset that I had to go back to my room. I've been there ever since.

If I don't get to work soon, I'm afraid I will lose my job. Then what will become of my parents and my sister? I need to get to the office. But every time I try to get out the door, I somehow end up sleeping or eating garbage.

I don't know how this condition came upon me. I don't want to make a fuss, so my plan is to just wait it out and hope everything goes back to normal soon. It can't last forever. Can it?

—Too Many Legs

Dear Legs:

Whatever this condition of yours may be, it does not sound like something that will just go away on its own. I suggest that you see a medical professional immediately. Your ailment is not something that I can help with. What I can help you with is exploring why getting help hasn't seemed to occur to you yet.

Why, Legs, have you not seen a doctor already? Is it a financial issue? You mentioned working a job you don't like to pay off the debts of your parents, which is already an unfair situation. Do you always put their needs before your own? You say your condition caused upset with your family, and your solution was to return to your room. But why didn't your family step in to help you? Did they even offer? Did you give them a chance to?

You strike me as one of those people who, for reasons both good and mistaken, have decided that you are responsible for the entire world. You believe that everybody is counting on you, that your role in life is to work hard to meet their expectations, and that disappointing them is the absolute worst thing you could possibly do. When people get in ruts like that, they forget that they are allowed to ask for what they need. They forget they're allowed to ask for help.

Have you asked your family to support you while you deal with your condition? Have you told your boss that you need time and space to heal? Have you said to anyone, anytime, anywhere, "I need your help?"

What might happen if you did?

—A. A.

Dear Aunt Antigone:

I'm being treated by a highly esteemed doctor, who has diagnosed me with a nervous condition and prescribed for me his "rest cure." At the behest of my physician, my husband and I have relocated to a large mansion in the country, where I have been instructed to refrain from any and all activities. He'd probably tell me that writing this message to you is doing too much—which is ironic, since I am a writer. (I'm composing this letter in secret while he's out, so as not to upset him.)

Do you have any idea how boring it is to do absolutely nothing? It's certainly not easing my distress. All I do is lie around and stare at the walls of my bedroom, which the previous owners covered with the most hideous yellow wallpaper. I have never viewed a more horrendous paper in my life!

The rest cure is challenging but I am determined to get better. John has been supportive, even though I get unreasonably angry with him sometimes. I can't fault him. He's also a doctor. He wholeheartedly believes in science, in evidence and proof; the hysterical cries of his overly emotional wife do not show up on any of his charts. He would never admit to this, but I'm beginning to believe he doesn't really think I'm sick. Oh, he says all the right things, but I can tell that he's holding back from sharing what he really feels. I suppose one must expect that in marriage.

What can I do to convince him that there really is something amiss with me? I'm sure I'd improve faster if I knew he believed it. I'll do anything to get better. (If only to get away from this wallpaper!)

—Climbing the Walls

Dear Climbing:

First, let me say that I believe you when you say that you're not well. Even if you cannot exactly put the words to what it is that you're feeling, the sense that something is wrong should always be listened to. Too often, we are expected to validate what we feel by describing it with only the prescribed words and concepts chosen by others. As if human understanding has effectively cataloged every type of event or emotion in the world.

You are a writer, so you may not be surprised to hear that words *are at the heart of your troubles. As supportive as you say your husband is, it's also evident that he doesn't listen to the words that you say to him. It's just as clear that you have resorted to choosing your words carefully, trying to make him hear you, which takes an enormous amount of energy—no wonder you're exhausted!*

I want to blame your husband and this doctor of yours—doing nothing? really?—but neither of them is the one who wrote to me. So, instead I give my advice to you, focusing on the things that you have under your control. And my counsel boils down to this: "speak up." Tell your husband how you feel using your own words, not his. Demand that he tell you what he really thinks, so you don't have to guess.

There's precious little honest communication happening between you two. Why do you think that is? Are you scared of what he might really believe? Are you worried you'll say the wrong thing? Are you trying to present yourself as a picture of what you think he wants, in order to keep him happy? Or are you scared that being your honest self will mean that your marriage can't continue as it has until now?

What would happen if you owned how you felt, if you said it loudly, unapologetically, or even if you demanded your feelings be taken seriously? Would it be disastrous if you didn't need validation by doctors to be allowed to feel how you really feel?

Worrying about the color of the wallpaper is a lot easier to do than letting your husband see you for who you truly are. I can't say doing that will cure your nervous condition. However, I'd bet it'll be more therapeutic than meekly staring at the walls and hoping you don't get caught writing.

Dear Aunt Antigone:

I have been shut up tight for the past several months along with a thousand of my closest courtiers and friends, while a terrible red plague burns across the land, striking down all the unfortunate wretches who cannot get out of its path. But we cannot be touched by it, safe as we are behind my fortified walls.

I will confess that the closeness and monotony has begun to wear. We are growing tired, bored, on edge. It is the responsibility of the nobility to care for their inferiors. And so, I would like to do something to ease the burdens of all those whom I am hosting in my abbey. But, given my station and their inferiority, I am having a devil of a time getting any of them to tell me what sort of activity would serve as a balm to their worries. They just tell me how dauntless and sagacious I am, and whatever I choose will be right. I love flattery as much as the next prince, but I'm trying to get a clear answer here!

Left to my own devices, I would opt for something magnificent and grand to stagger the senses. A masked ball! Each room bathed with light of a different color! Musicians! Dancers! Strolling mummers! No one could fail to have their spirits lightened by such a display! But then I wonder if that would be too much? If, given the current state of things, perhaps something more restrained and elegant would fit the mood.

Which is the better choice, Aunt Antigone? Sober and solemn, or delirious fancies such as the madman fashions?

—A Prosperous Prince

Dear Prince:

How noble and generous of you to care for the spirits of your—how did you put it?—"inferiors." I'm sure they do all call you dauntless and sagacious. I'm sure they also call you many other things when you are not there to hear them. You, a person of great power in your land, have chosen to insulate yourself and a few hundred hand-selected toadies behind fortified gates while a highly contagious disease infects everyone on the outside.

And you want to throw a party.

You speak of your responsibility. What about your responsibility to all of those outside your fortress? What about the unlucky ones who were not chosen by their prince? What is your responsibility to them? Perhaps you believe you have none. Perhaps you are of that class of people who believe that material wealth and fortune mean that they have been anointed by the gods as a superior being, that they stand above the rest. But no one, not a single one of us, can ever be that privileged.

You mention your gates—who is guarding them? Your musicians and mummers—do they share your esteem for yourself? Your courtiers—do they tell you what you want to hear even though in truth they despise you? Do you understand that it would only take one of them to decide that their little life is worth spending to end your great one, to open your gates and let that red plague in? Your rank, station, or fortune won't make any difference then—you'll be the wretch.

So, Prince, I don't think the kind of party you throw is

going to matter. Gaudy or restrained, wild or serious, you're just planning your own funeral. Instead I strongly suggest that you use your vast resources and power to help all those outside your gates who are suffering. I guarantee you that whichever you choose, you won't be plagued by boredom much longer.

—A. A.

Dear Aunt Antigone:

They all think I'm mad. But I'm not. I can see what is going to happen. It's a gift from the gods of Olympus. Although lately, it's become more of a curse.

I thought I could be helpful. I thought I could be of service. Who wouldn't want to know something about what the future holds, right? I told them all what I saw, and they praised my gift, made sacrifices to Apollo.

And then they totally ignored me. The more right I am, the less they listen. It doesn't matter how much I am proved correct, nobody seems to care. Nobody wants to hear bad news, ever. They like to blame the messenger. Especially when that messenger is me.

I thought I'd gotten used to it, the way they placate me and call me a madwoman behind my back. But now, I see doom on the horizon. Every person in our city is in great danger. I should tell them; I need to tell them all. But the thought of going through all of it again, of being ignored, mocked, belittled, and slighted—it just leaves me feeling exhausted.

They think I'm mad, and if I don't figure out a way to stop it from getting to me, I'm afraid I might actually lose my mind.

—Stressed Prophetess

Dear Stressed:

There are those who are mad, and those whom the world makes mad with its injustice and indifference. I know exactly which kind you are.

I also know a bit about the kind of situation you're in. Standing up and declaring a truth in the face of powerful men who feel their plans threatened—that's not a comfortable position. The gods can do whatever they want, but that doesn't mean men who believe they are gods should be obeyed the same way!

I also understand the impulse to take your toys and go home, to punish those who do not see things as you do. It can be hard in the position you are in to find a charitable outlook. But pity these poor men, so concerned with their puffed-up egos and their need to be right that they will allow an entire city to be destroyed rather than heed the advice of one woman.

Take comfort in this—if the outcome is preordained, if nothing you do can prevent the doom advancing on you, then you can liberate yourself from caring what people think about you. Tell everyone. Hold nothing back. For at this point, what's left for you to lose?

Dear Aunt Antigone:

I've been dismasted. A parmacetty of uncommon malice took my leg and left me scarred, broken, and teetering on the brink of madness. My crew saved my life, but it was a long voyage back from the Pacific and round the Cape. The entire time, I had to be confined to my quarters, bound and straitjacketed, weeping, wailing, raving. All I could think was, Why me? What did it want with me? What caused that white monstrosity to target me with such vengeance?

All the long months of the voyage home, I was consumed with thoughts of that monstrous creature. Every night I dreamed, and I saw myself jamming my harpoon into its milky eye, spewing gouts of crimson raining over the albino skin, conquering the beast. Every morning I woke, stump bleeding, and I wept. By the time the Pequod *arrived home in Nantucket months later, I was able to show my face to the world again. This outward show, however, is a lie. It is nothing more than a fiction I can maintain for short periods.*

I have a wife, poor girl, who married me when I was a different man. She can see right through my mask, and she knows that the person she shares her home with is an imposter. We have a young son, and the confusion on his face when he looks at the creature who occupies the shape of his father is enough to rend my spirit. I do not belong here anymore.

The leg is gone below the knee. But I can still feel it, heavy, burning, always. I have fashioned various devices that allow me to move about. Every step sends a lance of pain through me. I can never forget, not for a moment.

I have recently been approached by my old business partners. They want to know if I have healed enough to undertake another voyage. Knowing them, they probably think that being short of a leg means they would have to pay me less. But I care not for their coin any longer.

I sleep less and less. When I do, my dreams are again invaded by that Leviathan. It is still out there. I cannot forget and I cannot forgive. I cannot move without pain and I cannot stay still.

I should not go. But I cannot stay here either. What say ye? To ship or not to ship?

—Old Thunder

Dear Thunder:

You have survived an overwhelming, scarring experience. I am not surprised that you think of yourself as an entirely different person than you were before it happened. But you're not. You have all the same experiences in your head. Your wife and your son, I promise you, do not think of you as a different man. I'm not saying your distress isn't real, but that they are projections of your pain and trauma. The loss of a limb does not have to equal the loss of your whole self; it just constitutes a redefinition of that self.

It is natural, after something like this happens, to spend a lot of time trying not only to understand why but also to divine the physical and metaphysical forces that led to the event. Some people find themselves drawn into new religions, become uncommonly devout, and find explanations that they can use to make sense of all their experiences. Others turn their back on religion totally and find in that rejection the freedom to determine their own future. There are a million other points between those poles for you to choose, but what they all have in common is a "story." You are crying out for a story to explain how you got to the place you are. But whether providential or satanic, the story you choose will give you a framework to understand the new world you find yourself in.

And still there's another story you could choose to embrace, but it's not easy. It's the one that says there is no meaning to what happened to you. That you were just in the wrong place at the wrong time with the wrong fish. At first blush, you may recoil at this story, for it seems that it renders your suffering, your pain, your experiences, as also meaningless. But I would argue that it's the exact opposite—that by refusing to ascribe meaning to your battle with the great Leviathan, you free yourself from its lingering effects and you open yourself to reconnecting with all the good things in the world.

Ultimately, you get to decide whether or not your wife and son will be more real to you than this phantom fish. One of these choices will give to you, the other will take. Which will make you feel at one with yourself again?

Dear Aunt Antigone:

Have you ever heard the old poem that asks, "Tell me where is fancy bred, or in the heart or in the head?" I used to think that the answer was obviously the heart. But I am no longer so certain.

Recently, I suffered a terrible fall. Oh, it was completely my fault. It was to be our last day in Lyme, and we all went out for a final walk. I insisted we go down to the Cobb. You see, Aunt Antigone, there was a man in our party, and I was convinced I was in love with him. Captain W. was resolute, and he esteemed determination in others. Therefore, I styled myself as confident, bidding to keep his attentions. The more he obliged me, the larger and bolder I became. How foolhardy I was.

I wanted to overwhelm him, and so I leapt from the steps into his arms. Except, in my eagerness, I jumped too soon and so fell, smacking my head on the stones below. It was quite a dire circumstance. I am told that Captain W. was frozen in apprehension and that of all people, it was Miss E.'s resolve and quick thinking that was my salvation.

I had obviously seriously injured myself, as there was some question of whether I would ever wake up, but after a few days I did, and I have been recovering ever since. But the strangest thing happened upon waking—all of the feelings I had for my captain, for this man whom I thought powerful and dependable but who froze in the moment of my greatest need—those feelings were suddenly, strangely gone. It was as if all my affections for him belonged to a different version of myself, a person quite divorced from who I am now.

Meanwhile, my convalescence has given me the opportunity to make a better acquaintance with another man. I had known Captain B. before my accident, though he never made much of an impression on me. And yet now, I can think of little else than a future with him.

Can it be that our personalities, our feelings, our very heart's desires, are so unfixed? Does it only require a blow to the head to change everything we think of ourselves? As much as I want to trust the feelings I now have for Captain B., what is to prevent some other injury from persuading me that I love still yet another?

—Hardheaded, Softhearted

Dear Hardheaded:

We all live in our heads. Our feelings, beliefs, ideals, all the things we consider when we discuss "character" belong to our minds. And then we go out into the world, and it changes us. This happens to everybody, although clearly you have had a much more dramatic experience of this than most.

You fear that your change of heart comes from the injury you've sustained. But is it possible that something more complex is happening? With your first captain, you identified the characteristics that he seemed attracted to, and so made an effort to display those qualities where he could see them. I'm curious why you assume that was more the "real" you than who you are now, when it could be argued that it was more the counterfeit. Is it possible that the injury jarred you out of feeling the need to fulfill the expectations of someone else, and instead made you feel more keenly the value of being yourself?

As to the possibility that some future episode could change your feelings again, I would say that it is a given. The world never stops affecting us, dear. But then again, we never stop affecting the world either, do we? Make your choices how you feel today, and leave tomorrow to that future version of yourself.

Dear Aunt Antigone:

I have the best job, the best designer wardrobe, the best friends, the best apartment building, the best drugs, the best morning skin routine, and the best taste. My handmade suits are spotless. I can do pretty much whatever I want. I often do. And there's nothing to stop me. I've left a trail of bodies behind me and nobody cares. But most of the time, I feel absolutely nothing, like I'm empty inside.

Then something will happen. I will catch a glimpse of someone else's business card and know instantly that their choice of font and card stock renders mine pathetic and laughable. Or I will realize that I forgot to return a videotape, and be consumed with shame and self-loathing. I'll become overwhelmed by the feeling that everything is out of control, and that I could disappear from the face of the earth and it wouldn't matter one bit. Before I know it, I'm on the verge of frenzy.

No one believes me. Not my "friends" or my fiancée or my mistress. If I try to tell them, they just laugh at me and assume I'm joking. I can't even tell what is real and what is imaginary anymore. I feel like I'm trapped in a fun house. How do I find the exit?

—Simply Not There

Dear Simply:

I'd guess it would be difficult for many people to have sympathy for you. You're surrounded by plenty, blessed with gifts that many will never have, and it all means nothing to you. You have a gaping hole in the center of your soul, and you're stuffing it with everything and anything you can get your hands on.

You don't feel anything because that would require making yourself vulnerable. So you protect yourself with your long list of "bests," as if they can keep you safe. But you know it won't work. There is no exit. There is no way to escape, because the thing you're trying to escape from is yourself, and your own sense of imperfection. To do that, you've split yourself in two, dissociated your emotional core from the armored, unfeeling exterior.

Instead of stumbling through the fun house looking for the way out, try stopping and sitting down on the floor. Place your hands across the carpet. How does it feel on your fingers? Describe it to yourself. What color is it? What texture? Feel the fabric of that handmade suit of yours. What does it feel like? Think of the actual sensation of it, not the name of who designed it, or the idea of its status, or how you think it makes you look to someone else. You may live in a world of luxury, but you don't feel any of it.

What might happen if you allowed yourself to actually feel all these things? Might you be able to let go of the never-ending drive to gorge yourself? To reintegrate the fractured pieces of your psyche? To value the sensations and experiences for themselves, instead of how they rate on some abstract list of the "best"?

But if you really have left a trail of bodies behind you, then perhaps the best place for you to learn how to reassemble yourself is under the care of professionals, in a safe, confined space where you can't hurt anyone else.

Dear Aunt Antigone:

I'm dying. I know it. My family knows it. It's inevitable.

My family has always placed a high value on charity, and from a young age, my sisters and I were taught to always think about those who had less than we did. So years ago, I was helping a poor family nearby, and I caught scarlet fever. I almost died, but I somehow recovered. But I was never the same after that.

I've known since ever I can remember that my time on this Earth would be short. I have tried to spend this time as well as I could, spreading happiness and goodwill, not causing strife. My family thinks of me as an angel, and I can see the grief in their eyes as they prepare for their lives without me. One of my sisters is a writer, and I can already see her starting to compose the tale of her poor, doomed sister.

But there are things that I have not told them. And I have to tell them to someone. I hope it's all right if I tell them to you.

I'm so angry. I'm so angry all the time, and I can never tell anyone or show anyone. It's not fair. I did everything I was told. I was kind and generous and charitable, and I helped the sick and the poor and I was obedient, and I never got in trouble, I was never cross. I never did anything, while my sisters were able to live, to fall in love, to travel to New York and Paris. And now I'm going to die before I get a chance to do anything.

My family are all going to be in so much pain after I go, and I do not want to add to their burdens. So I'm trying to hold it all in. But if I never tell them, will they have ever known the real me?

—Little Piano

Dear Piano:

I am so sorry for your situation. I will spare you the platitudes and homilies, and just say that it would be a shame if you passed on without the people who love you getting to see the real you.

Your family have cast you in the role of a character who only grows more beautiful and saintlier as she gets sicker. You say your sister is a writer; very well, she can write about that character as much as she likes later on. But while you have your own time left, you are entitled to use it however you see fit.

So, scream, cry, break things, create a spectacle, make demands, carry on. Or sit quietly and watch the birds if you want. It's your time, you don't owe it to anyone else.

Chapter 5

BONDS *of* MATRIMONY

People get married for many different reasons. No matter why or how they choose their life partners, the result is often the same: an intimacy that is inseparable from vulnerability. Nobody can hurt you quite like a spouse can. A marriage requires joining your own needs to someone else's, often denying yourself what you want and holding your tongue when everything in you yearns to speak. It requires constant negotiation, frequent conflict, and a lot of pain.

Marriage is a promise, but it is also a contract. It's the yoking of two separate souls into a single unit. This doesn't happen without struggle. Some are not cut out for it. Others pine for it, only to regret it later. And it is never, ever, easy. But while marriage can cause struggle, heartache, and pain, we humans keep doing it. So it must be worth it, right? I'll confess, I never married. I came close though. I wish I'd had the opportunity, but larger forces intervened. Instead of a wedding, Haemon and I had funerals. And don't get me started on my father's marriage.

The letters I get about marriage are often from people looking for someone to take their side in an argument that they're having with their spouse. I can't always just write back, "talk to them instead of me," even if that is a universally applicable prescription. Of course, that assumes they can admit to themselves what they truly want. Often, it's easier to pick a fight than it is to honestly answer that question. Therefore, I also tell them to have a hard conversation with themselves. Often, that's where the real conflict lies.

Dear Aunt Antigone:

My husband has just received a great advance in his—well, our—fortunes. And yet, it's clear to me that his vaulting ambition could be gratified if he would undertake one slight deed, which some might deem ill in the eyes of Heaven. (After all, a king is anointed in the eyes of God.) But to me, this undertaking is a mere trifle. And by weird tongues, we are assured of its success.

It is unfortunate that my husband, though practiced in the arts of war, is often too filled with the milk of human kindness. I have traded my milk for gall, and I would perform the deed myself, if it were possible.

However, as the hour grows near, my brain is seized with thoughts of mercy. Shall I release my husband from his vow or use my venomous and valorous tongue to rouse him to action? I fear that our partnership cannot succeed unless one of us screws our courage to the sticking place.

—Invested in Inverness

Dear Invested:

Long and storied is the history of women taking the reins in times of crisis. You should see some of the flawed men in my family, and the ways that I had to force them to do The Things That Needed to Be Done. Of course, when they succeeded, they won all the glory. And when it failed, I took the blame.

Just how "slight" is this deed? If it seems minor to you, why is it such a big issue for your husband? Does this bring up differences in your worldviews, your values, and ethics? In ambitious partnerships, each spouse can spur the other to great heights. But you have to make sure that you're both clear on what you're risking, and what you hope to gain. Because one slight deed easily leads to the next, and the next. And once your hands are even a little bit dirty, it can be murder to get them clean.

If your husband has honest misgivings, forcing him into action is not a good strategy for long-term happiness in the marriage. Likewise, take stock of your own reasons. Is this what you really want? Sometimes it's easy to reflexively take a contrary position, especially if the argument is masking a deeper conflict. If you're like me, you've even found yourself arguing for something that you're not sure if you even really want. Sometimes, the argument takes over everything else.

But backing down from a fight doesn't mean you're not strong. It just means you've decided what is most important to you. And sometimes real strength is the ability to not *move forward, to look at what you have and decide that it's enough. Can you be satisfied with what you have now? If not, then ask yourself just how little this transgression will seem once it can't be taken back. Can you do it and sleep well? Or might it come back to haunt you?*

Dear Aunt Antigone:

I met the most wonderful man in Monte Carlo. Others seem to feel that he's distant, cold even. But I can feel the heart beating inside of him. After a whirlwind courtship, we were married and he brought me back to his home, a grand estate that took my breath away. But not long after we arrived, things started to go awry.

I knew that he had been married previously, but he didn't tell me much about his first wife other than that she'd died in a terrible boating accident. But when I arrived, it was quickly made clear to me how much everyone in the house and the local society worshipped this woman. Everything I do is seen as inferior to her and her greatness. My husband doesn't seem to think there's anything wrong, but I find myself feeling more and more isolated.

I do not wish to insult the memory of the departed or offend the sensibilities of those in my new home. But I am at a loss for how to continue, especially with the household staff. The housekeeper in particular troubles me. I thought she was there to help me, but I'm beginning to suspect she might have ulterior motives. Frankly, she's beginning to scare me. And I fear that my husband may be beginning to regret our quick marriage, and bringing me here to Manderley.

Please, Aunt Antigone, tell me, how can I make this house a home?

—Little Fool

Dear Little:

You are undoubtedly in a difficult position. A wedding doesn't only mean you're marrying your husband, but you're also getting everything he brings with him—family, old relationships, a way of life, a worldview. Ideally, this is an equitable exchange—each partner brings their entire history to the new relationship. But in your case, the scales seem unfairly balanced, as you are shedding most of your old life to immerse yourself into your husband's world. It is bound to be a rough transition.

The fact that you are succeeding someone who made a large impression can only compound the situation. You are flesh and blood, which means you have needs that may not be convenient, opinions that may not be enjoyed, and can make mistakes that can be enumerated. Because she is dead, the impulse for many will be to only see her good qualities and to forget about her flaws. But you can bet she had them, and if you can outlast the drive to only think the best of her, you should start to see the scales tip in your favor. Do not give up so quickly. Stay there. Fight for what you want. Make your husband remember why he married you in the first place. Do whatever you must to build something new with him, and if this estate is haunted by his first wife, then take him somewhere else. You're alive, and so is he. Do not let a dead woman decide the fate of your marriage.

No matter what else, consider replacing that housekeeper. You deserve to feel comfortable in your own home and she certainly doesn't seem like she has your best interests at heart.

—*A.A.*

Dear Aunt Antigone:

I am not a good man. I know this. I am ill-tempered, moody, and difficult. I made many mistakes in my youth, one of them irrevocable. I have been made to pay—and I continue to pay for them to this day. I had long given up the thought of finding any true happiness in this world. Until she *arrived as a governess for my ward. She is a pale little elf. I see her tremble when I loom over her. And yet, she neither flinches nor recoils.*

I have treated her cruelly; I have mocked and toyed and manipulated and hurt her. I have even counterfeited that I was intended to marry someone else. And still, she looked at me like she was the only one who could see my true self. Then, just when this mocking changeling had wormed her way into my soul, abruptly she left. She hastened to visit some sick aunt that treated her abominably, and yet she rushed off to care for her. I could not dissuade her from going. How she clings to those who mistreat her.

She is gone, and I am in torment. If—when—*she returns, I mean to drop the pretense and ask her to marry me. I know that I shouldn't, that there are a million reasons why we cannot be married—the laws of man and God and society stand in the way. But damn them all, I have suffered enough. For Jane, I will wash my hands of the world's judgment, defy man's opinion.*

My whole life, I have done what others expected of me, and it has cost me dearly. Do I have to pay for my mistakes forever? Or do I get to be happy for once?

—The Very Devil

Dear Devil:

I believe you when you say you are tormented. I believe that you feel like you have suffered for a long time. And yes, everybody deserves to be happy. But I must confess some unease—not at the lines you've written, but at the spaces in between.

You say "the laws of man and God and society stand in the way" of you marrying your little elf girl. But you omit any useful details. You would be far from the first man to fall for a pretty young thing in your employ. While certain quarters frown on romantic relationships arising under such conditions, that would hardly seem to rise to the levels of societal rejection as you anticipate.

So, what else is the problem? I find it quite telling that you do not describe it. You obliquely hint at it, as if it's something you think about constantly but never allow yourself to acknowledge. Perhaps it is related to your youthful irrevocable mistake? I can't but wonder what it is. Perhaps a previous marriage gone awry? Your words have all the pain of someone who has survived an ill-chosen marriage and not been able to put it behind them. Have you told your changeling about it? Have you told her anything at all? Are you intending to propose to this girl without revealing all of the heavy things that weigh on your heart? I wager that you'll wait until the last possible second to tell her the truth. Do you think that is kind? Is that the act of someone in love? Or someone who is grasping for control?

I have bad news for you, Devil. The intensity of your passion does not make up for the impurity of your intent. In fact, the more intensely you declare your love, the more you display your true faithlessness. You'll never be happy unless you own up to your mistakes, unless you embrace them and let her—and the world—see you for who you really are. It means making yourself vulnerable. It means submitting yourself for judgment, not defying it. You have to risk her seeing it all and rejecting you. But if she does choose to marry you still, then you will have earned your happiness.

Until then, you're just lying to her and everyone else. No one should marry under false pretenses. If you try to make her do so, then you're absolutely correct—you are not a good man.

Dear Aunt Antigone:

I recently took a trip to Moscow and met someone, a cavalryman. He stirred something profound in me. I did not sleep a wink on the train home. My mind was filled with indecorous, illicit thoughts of him, thoughts that I've never had before. I kept telling myself that when I got back to St. Petersburg, to my husband and my son, I would be able to forget him.

When I got off the train, my husband was waiting for me. The moment I saw him, my heart sank. It was like I had never really seen him before. His sagging skin, his crooked teeth. The way he talks to me like he's always laughing at my expense. His ears. My God, how I hate his ears.

And just then, coming off the same train, my dashing cavalryman appeared. The introductions were polite, the conversation appropriate, and yet the intent in his eyes was unmistakable. I was consumed by two equal and opposing desires—for him to leave me alone and never set eyes on me again, and for him to whisk me away right there, carry me back to the train and away from St. Petersburg. The whole time, I watched my husband's cold eyes, the slice of his cruel mouth, convinced that he could read every thought on my face.

Finally, the count left us, promising to visit soon. How I long for and dread that day! Then Alexei Alexandrovich sent me on home—alone, of course, while he went to one of his endless committee meetings. During the carriage ride home, I was consumed with only one thought, I think I hate my husband.

What can I do to escape these feelings? If the count does come calling, I'm afraid I won't be able to resist him.

—Restrained on a Train

Dear Restrained:

I could write you an exegesis on how marriages are long, and the things you once found charming about your spouse, through long familiarity, can easily become detestable. I could exhort you to remain faithful to your commitments, to disdain the flush of new attraction for a stable foundation. But I won't. Because you know all these things already.

You say you want to escape your feelings for this dashing young man, but I think you're really asking for permission. For absolution. To have your desires confirmed, to feel justified in your pursuit of an illicit romance outside of your marriage. I can't give you that. But you don't really need my blessing. Remain faithful or break your vows, hew to social norms or flout them, pursue passion or duty—you're going to do whatever you want to. Just don't blame your husband for it.

That hatred you think you feel is just a way for you to put aside your own responsibility. It seems to me that you feel that if your unhappiness is his fault, then it justifies you taking whatever action you need to make yourself happy. While you may have many disagreements and disappointments in your marriage, it's up to you to address them with him. Anything else is tantamount to running away. And when you get in the habit of running away from your problems, what are you going to do when they catch up to you? You can't run forever.

—*A.A.*

Dear Aunt Antigone:

My wife is the most beautiful woman in the world. I know many husbands think that of their women, but in her case it's the truth. But I wish it weren't so, for it has caused no end of grief.

Years ago, she left me. She swears that she didn't mean to hurt me, that she got caught up in events beyond her control, that she was compelled by the gods. I don't know all the details of everything that happened—the stories are wildly different depending on who you talk to. But I know too much and know her too well to believe that she was wholly innocent. And I saw the way she looked at him, stood by his side in front of everyone. On some level, she knew what she was doing.

Nevertheless, I fought to get her back. I moved the Heavens and the Earth. I did not rest until my queen was back at my side. Finally, she came home, and I accepted her back. We attempted to move past our troubles, if only for the sake of our children.

But as much as I want to put her betrayal, the wars, and all of the damage behind us, my heart is unquiet. What if it happens again? How do I know that, the moment I turn my back, she won't run off with some other hero?

Will I ever really be able to trust her again?

—Spartan Husband

Dear Spartan:

When a marriage ruptures—whether from infidelity, abandonment, or even the games of the gods—the process of rebuilding it can take a very long time. Hearing of your trials and tribulations, I know that you must have many wounds, not all of them readily visible. You can't force them to heal at the pace you would like—they will take however much time they need. And though in your telling, you are the aggrieved party, you can be sure that your wife bears her own deep, difficult scars.

Your unease is sensible. Once you feel someone has betrayed you, you can't help but wonder if they might do it again. In the back of your mind, there's always a question about if there's a hidden knife, just waiting to come out and stab you in the back once more.

I can hear that you are still angry. That you have accepted her back is magnanimous of you. But it is only the first step on a long road toward rebuilding trust. And while your uncertainty is focused on your wife and her actions, in reality you are the one with the choice in this situation. You have to decide which means more to you —restoring your marriage or holding on to your anger, your sense of injustice.

Before you reflexively answer this question, swearing that you will do whatever is necessary to restore peace to your union, take a moment to search your heart. Because threaded throughout your story is a tone of righteous indignation. You have been wronged! She wronged you! You have undertaken labors almost as great as Heracles's to win her back. You have earned it. You have proven yourself the better man.

Now you need to forget all of that. Because every time you indulge your anger and indignation, you are telling your wife that whatever pain she feels, she deserves. And maybe you think that she does. That's a perfectly reasonable stance to take. Just understand that those beliefs are the very thing that stands in the way of your marriage being able to move on.

You may think you have forgiven her, but I don't think you really have. That's understandable. It will take a long time. But that's work that only you can do. You may not want to do that work, but in those moments when you think it's too much to ask, remind yourself that the gods always demand sacrifices. Sometimes that's a burnt offering, and sometimes that's your own pride.

Dear Aunt Antigone:

My husband is a powerful and influential man. He relies on me to host social events for the important people in his circle, and it is a role that I have adapted to well. Last night was one such party. The prime minister was in attendance, as were many other important people who are influential in government, society, and business. Needless to say, this party took a tremendous amount of work on my part. But as his wife, this is my function, and while it might not seem to be that important in the grand scheme of events, he assures me that it is crucial to his work. Most of the time, I am content with that. But last night was an exception. At several instances during the evening, I was convinced that the whole affair might be a disaster.

You see, earlier in the day, rather out of nowhere, I was called upon at home by someone from my past. Someone who was once very important to me. Who even once wanted to marry me. He burst in today, back after five years in India. And there were so many things flurrying in my mind, I could not tell what I really felt. My throat was so stiff I could barely get the words out. He announced that he was in love—not with me, of course—and then suddenly burst into tears. Before I knew what I was doing, I leaned over and kissed him. He pulled away and went to the window—he polished that absurd knife that he always carries. For a minute, I imagined running off with him, and then the next second the fancy passed. Then my daughter came into the room and he left abruptly. As he was going, I blurted out that he should come to the party. I haven't a clue why I did that.

He did come. I did my best to avoid him. But then she

arrived. She'd lost some of her luster, if I'm being honest. Having five boys will do that. But when we were at Bourton, I remember I would do anything just to be near her. Hadn't that been love too? But last night, it was like it'd never happened. We spoke of things that didn't matter. I pulled myself away as soon as I could. After all, the prime minister had to be seen to. I had duties.

But how strange it is that both these persons from my past returned on the same day to remind me of how different my life turned out from how I'd imagined it would. Toward the end of the evening, I looked at my husband and was filled with shame and remorse. Did I make a terrible mistake marrying him? Have I betrayed my younger self, her dreams and ideals and passions? Will this regret ever go away?

—A Hostess

Dear Hostess:

Old friends and old loves cause a particular kind of ache. You can go years without seeing them or speaking, and suddenly you're near them again, and your whole body remembers the closeness that was once there. Even if you don't want it to. Some intimacies can never be forgotten. Some business can never be finished.

But really, it's easy to look at what you have all around you and feel contempt. You are confronted with its reality, its flaws, every day. It's understandable that all you can see of the road not taken is your idealization of it. So I ask, would you at this moment, trade everything you have for a different version of the world where you made different choices? Or would you trade everything you have now for anything else, *no matter what it is?*

In any respect, you might try to find more compassion for yourself. All of us are changed by the world and the experiences that we have in it. All of us would be disappointments to our younger selves, who loved so intensely and so fearfully, who were so petrified of the magic of life and of loss.

You aren't that person anymore. None of us are. But you're still breathing. Though you may be different than who you were then, you can also be a different person tomorrow, if you take the plunge. The question is: Are you willing to take it?

Dear Aunt Antigone:

I am newly married to an elegant man. He is so refined that I sometimes cannot believe he would even be interested in me. He is a Frenchman, dark and romantic, and there's no one else like him in our quiet little New England town. I fell for him the moment he turned up on my doorstep, in need of a room to rent, as if fate had brought us together.

It took me a long time to work up the nerve to confess my love to him. I prayed to God for guidance, and He told me to write him a letter baring my true feelings. Of course, I expected him to spurn me, to tear my letter to shreds and consign it the vortex of the toilet. But, mon Dieu, *I was wrong! Hum wanted to get married right away, and that was fine with me. I didn't want him to have a chance to change his mind. Also, I wanted it done before my daughter came back from camp. Dolores can be so negativistic and obstinate. She delights in tormenting me, and I could not risk her doing something to drive Hum away.*

These weeks of wedded bliss have been among the happiest of my life. And yet, there is something dogging me, and I can't quite put my finger on what it is. I get the sense he is hiding things from me. Sometimes, he'll get very quiet, as if he is following some complex train of thought. But when I ask him what he's thinking, he always makes up some story that I know isn't true.

We turned his old bedroom into a writer's den, and in there he has a table with a locked drawer. When I asked him what was inside, he teased me by saying "love letters." He does not know how much this wounded me, even in jest. Dolores will be returning home from camp soon, and I find that I cannot stop thinking about what is in that drawer. Married folk should share everything with each other, shouldn't they? I can't imagine what secrets he's keeping that would change how I feel about him.

I was moving some furniture around, trying to spruce the place up, and I found the key to the drawer. It has taken every inch of my self-possession to keep from using it to discover what's inside. I know that I shouldn't look at his things without his permission. But man and wife are supposed to share everything! I have no secrets from him. And as his wife, aren't I entitled to know what he's hiding?

—Missus H

Dear Missus H:

If you feel that your husband is keeping something important from you, then you are well within your rights to ask him to explain. But a clear violation of his boundaries such as opening his locked drawer would not seem like an auspicious start to the relationship.

You are still new to each other, still negotiating how you live your days as a family unit. There are all kinds of marriages, ones where the couple tells each other every tiny thing, others where they prefer to keep most of their spheres separate, still others which function more as business relationships than love matches. Have you and your husband discussed what your marriage will be? If not, I fear that your ideal may be radically different from his.

What does your intuition tell you? I'll tell you what mine says: a hasty marriage, a man who keeps secrets and a locked drawer—these signs do not point to a happy outcome.

If you open that drawer, are you prepared for what you might discover?

Dear Aunt Antigone:

I've been in love with a woman for a long time. She is the queen of my heart. After years of waiting for the right time, I was finally able to marry her. Now, every day is a celebration. The canons roar, the wine flows, the revels are endless. We are making up for all the time we missed, living every day to its fullest. It's all that I hoped for. There's only one complication.

My wife has a son from a previous marriage. I've tried to make it clear to him that I will treat him as if he were my own, and I've taken pains to include him in as much as possible. But no matter what I do, he shows me nothing but contempt. At first, he just refused to be civil, moping around and glaring at me all the time. Lately, he's begun to act out, behaving erratically and intentionally causing all kinds of trouble. I am a public figure, and I can't afford to have him keep undermining me like this. I was prepared for some friction, of course. I have dealt with him fairly and openly, but the clouds still hang on him and he refuses to behave reasonably.

I have tried to talk to my wife about this, but in her eyes her son can do no wrong. If only he would see that he has nothing to fear from me, all would be well. But this has been going on for two months now, and my patience is wearing thin. How much longer must I allow him to insult me like this before I am justified in retaliating? How can I convince my wife to see how rotten his behavior is?

—Great Uncle

Dear Uncle:

I'm curious about what made this the "right time" for you to marry your wife. Was her previous husband still in the picture until then? If that's the case, then your new stepson is likely still grieving the end of his parents' relationship. That grief will take its own time. In your excitement to finally enjoy the fruits of your new marriage, is it possible that you have not given him enough time? Two whole months, and you expect him to accept you with open arms?

You say you had to wait for your wife for a long time. Did you hide your feelings for her as well as you think you did? Perhaps your stepson has known your true motives toward his mother for longer than you care to acknowledge. Did his father know? Were you sneaking around with your wife before *she was your wife? Because even if you think nobody knew . . . somebody knew. Even if he didn't have the facts, I'll wager your stepson bristled every time you entered the room, sensing your intentions.*

I'll level with you—it's possible that your stepson never gets over this. Convincing your wife to take your side against a son that she dotes on does not seem to be a battle you will enjoy fighting. You can't go back and change the past. It doesn't sound like you would, even if you could. This new marriage has made you very happy, so your stepson's ongoing opposition may just have to be the price you pay for that happiness. Are you willing to pay it?

Chapter 6

The WAY WE WORK

While I am generally content with my lot in life, occasionally I will succumb to the passing fancy of dreaming of what I might have become were my circumstances different. I might have liked to become a lawyer or an artist. A doctor or a professor. But where I grew up, there really weren't any "jobs" or "professions" like there are in modern times. So these were never options for me.

Every society has different rules surrounding work—who gets to do it, who gets the rewards, what work is valued, and what is overlooked. But regardless of what we "do" day in and day out, ambition drives us, and often torments us when we feel we fall short of our goals. Some of us sacrifice large portions of our lives in pursuit of advancing ourselves in our given field. Others spend their lives merely looking for the chance to do what they aspire to, and are continuously thwarted by chance or belief, by custom or temperament, by fear or caution.

We all look for meaning and purpose through the work we do, and how it affects the world around us. But if that meaning eludes us, it can be as painful as any lost love or shattered dreams.

Dear Aunt Antigone:

I have always wanted to be a great artist. When I was younger, I tried my hand at many different types of art—drawing, sketching, oils, charcoal. Recently, I traveled to Paris as a companion for my wealthy aunt, and I have been concentrating on painting. I thought I was getting quite good at it.

But then, on a sojourn to Rome, I was confronted with an irrefutable fact: I am not, after all, a genius. I may possess some talent and energy, but these are no substitute for true genius and never can be. And now I feel stupid for even trying. One of my sisters is a genius—she is even able to support herself with her literary talents—but I am decidedly not. And if I can't be great, then I don't want to be anything.

I'm thinking that I should quit art altogether. Stop wasting time on dreaming for an impossible career, and accept the affection of a wealthy man. But if I do that, have I wasted all of these years? Have I made a fool of myself in the process?

—Common-Place Dauber

Dear Dauber:

My, you're hard on yourself, aren't you? Your all-or-nothing attitude is extreme, and it's an impossible standard for anybody to live up to. Any young painter who compares their work to that of the masters hanging in the galleries of Rome is doomed to be disappointed.

The problem with genius is that nobody can tell what it is when they first see it. Genius isn't a quality—it's a consensus. It's a question of numbers. If enough people decide something is genius, then it is. But no matter what they decide, if you're the one making the artwork, then you're the one person who doesn't get a vote in the matter.

Where did you get the idea that you should only be allowed to paint if you're a genius? If you could free yourself of that impossible standard, would you be more content with the work you are creating?

When you are painting and drawing, do you enjoy what you are doing? To me, that is the only question worth considering. If you do not derive pleasure from the process, if it does not call to you in some way, then why pursue it as a career at all? But if you despair because what you make doesn't seem good enough, then the answer is to keep making new works, not quitting when it gets difficult.

I don't think any of the years you've spent could be considered a waste. Especially not if you've derived your own meaning from it. But I expect that the real trouble you are facing is that your own approval isn't enough. You need the validation of someone else. That's not unusual, as we all need to be seen and loved and praised. Reading between the lines, it seems that you are seeking that approval from your sister, who may not be ready to give it to you and from whom you may not feel able to accept it. Either way, you will not get to the bottom of the matter by quitting.

Besides, as a society, we place too much of a premium on genius anyway. There are a lot of levels in between "great" and "nothing," including "very good" and "excellent" and "worth the effort." Might you find a way to be content with one of those? Devoting yourself to producing art of that caliber is hardly a waste of time.

And might you find someone whose praise you would find a little bit easier to attain?

—A.A.

Dear Aunt Antigone:

In my work as a doctor, I have laboured to discover scientific truths that would further man's knowledge of our world, and hopefully relieve the sorrow and suffering of the masses. To all, my public countenance is one of gravity, sober deliberation, and respectability. But in truth I have always found the life of study to be dry, my work to be unsatisfying.

You see, as I have reached the years of reflection, I find that I have had for much of my life been filled with desires for other kinds of experiences, pleasures that might not be suitable to discuss in polite company. I have repressed these yearnings and tried to embody all the characteristics of the gentleman scientist. But this repression has not extinguished my desires; in fact, it has only made them keener.

My scientific labor verges on the mystic and transcendental. Of late it has served only to highlight for me the perennial war that is continuously taking place amongst the various parts of my consciousness. At times, I feel that I am not one man, but two. By chance, I have stumbled upon certain drugs that might be able to help bring out the expression of the more natural, less repressed side of my nature. And yet, as much as I crave the release of parts of me long repressed, I hesitate to consume these medicines.

Work, service, duty—these are the ideals held up by our society. I have spent a lifetime seeming to embody the spirit of them. But if I were to indulge the secret parts of my psyche, would that strike a balance between my constituent parts? Or is that merely rejecting those social goods in favor of selfish self-

gratification? Can there ever be some accord between my work and my inner life?

—Out of Balance

Dear Balance:

On the surface, you are right—a lifetime spent working at a vocation at the expense of what brings you joy is no recipe for happiness. Too often we repress the things that call to our souls, trading them instead for money, esteem, public or private approval. On the other hand, there is a long and storied tradition of abandoning one's established career in search of something that truly fulfills you. I wish I could tell you that following that path would lead you to happiness. But to be honest, Balance, there are a few things you mention that give me pause.

Perhaps it's your use of the word pleasures, *which conjures up some kind of orgiastic, sybaritic abandonment of restraint or sense? Or maybe it's your fixation on some drug you've discovered in your lab, as if it is the key to unlocking your true self. Are you seeking permission to take it? Or preemptive absolution for what you do under its influence?*

In the abstract, we like to believe self-repression causes pain and suffering. But is that true for all *self-repression? Or do we all have things inside of us that need to be repressed for the safety of society? Balance is a laudable ideal, but sometimes it can be used to justify indulgences. I surmise that it all depends on what those "pleasures" really are. Are they perfectly natural desires that some societies have clamped down on in ignorance, fear, or oppression? Or are they the kinds of transgressions that every society would find abhorrent? The logic of "balance" can be used to explain both cases.*

Right now, these questions are theoretical. But should you choose to move forward and release your shadow self, the matter will become real, as will any consequences of what you do in your "liberated" state. When the drugs wear off, you may have to decide who you really are.

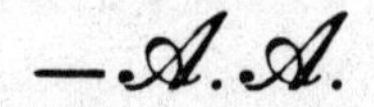

Dear Aunt Antigone:

This rich old white man gave me a job as a chauffeur. He said he was a supporter of the NAACP and wanted to help me. I don't feel comfortable in his big house, but Mama keeps telling me that with the money I make, we could move somewhere better, someplace that didn't have rats. All I know about rich white folks is what I see in the movies.

He has a daughter. I don't like her. I don't like the way she looks right at me. The way she talks to me—like we're the same—for some reason it just makes me see red. She's got a man, and he's a Communist. I don't like him one bit.

Everybody has been nice to me and that just scares me more. They even have a white servant, and she told me that they let their last chauffeur go to night school and now he's got a nice government job. So maybe if I do it long enough, I could get myself into a better situation. I guess I really am lucky to have a chance like this. It'd be nice to get away from the rats.

So why do I feel like I should run away from these people as far as I can?

—Son of Chicago

Dear Chicago:

Instincts are funny, aren't they? When things appear like they should be good, they can feel wrong. When everything is terrible, there can be a sudden lightness of spirit. It's confusing when our hearts and our heads disagree.

It would be easy for me to say that you should trust your instincts, that you should run, that you should put as much distance between yourself and these people as you can. From the little you've said, it would appear that none of them see you as a person, but as a vessel, an emblem, a symbol of how enlightened they are. They do not have your best interest at heart.

It would be easy for me to say that, but I won't. Because we can't always choose for ourselves. The world puts us in a particular place at a particular time and tries to convince us that we are the authors of our own destiny—but in reality, the place and time do much to shape what we even think is possible.

If you think there's another route for advancement that would not cause you so many misgivings, then take that if you can. But if you feel you must stick it out in this job, don't ignore those instincts. Make sure your eyes stay open. Step carefully, and perhaps you can find a way through it.

Dear Aunt Antigone:

My boss is an addled old man. When he asked me to work with him, I only agreed because he promised to make me the governor of my own island. I am a poor farmer, and the only thing I could ever hope to govern before this was my own ass. After all your belly leads your feet, not the other way around!

So I went along with him. Even though everybody told me he was mad. Now, I think sometimes that everyone was right, and I should try to get my boss to see the real world in front of us. But other times, he believes his delusions so strongly that I almost start to see them myself!

I am not sure what to do about him. What's more important when dealing with your employer—truth or loyalty?

—Proverbial Sidekick

Dear Proverbial:

We all know people who believe strange things. Of course, sometimes we are those people.

There's a famous proverb about flies and honey, as I'm sure you know. The conclusion it draws applies to your situation. Telling someone they're mad will not make them suddenly reconsider their deeply held beliefs. Even if they are delusions. Especially *if they are delusions. It will only make them firmer in their convictions.*

The truth is certainly a good thing, but truth can never be forced on someone who does not want to recognize it. You can lead a donkey to water, but if he doesn't want to go, he'll fight you the whole way.

But what if your donkey is dying of thirst and still doesn't want to move? Will yelling at him make him budge? Beating him? Trying to demonstrate to him the error of his ways? Or do you allow him to walk where he wants and slowly try to nudge him in the direction you wish him to go?

Sometimes, getting to the water means first going away from the water. Is that truth or delusion? It's hard to tell when you're in the middle. What does your gut tell you? I suggest you follow that.

Dear Aunt Antigone:

For as long as I can remember, I have felt called to do something extraordinary, to complete some great work that will have an impact in the world. In my pursuit of this, I have often been met with resistance, disinterest, or outright mockery. Apparently, young gentlewomen are not meant to undertake any work of importance. But I do believe one ought to strive for greatness, and to make the world a better place for one's fellow man, in spite of those challenges.

When I met my husband, I thought I had found a way to contribute my energies toward a project that could have a real effect. He is engaged in what can only be described as a Great Work, divining a key that will uncover the single source of all of the world's disparate mythologies. He is a clergyman and knows so much of the world and its history, and I began to imagine all that I could learn from him. While he wrote his book, I would eagerly assist him, organizing his research, and in the process pursuing my own studies. I hoped that in this way, I could learn everything about the world and become a scholar. It would have been a fulfillment of all my aspirations.

But once we were married, I discovered that Edward was not interested in my help. He regards all of that studying and education that I was so keen on as an interruption to his work. Any opinion I venture is received as criticism and censure. My offers of assistance have been spurned. I am left alone, idle, and purposeless.

Have I been a fool to think I could play some part in any

kind of Great Work? Am I doomed to live a meaningless life in which nothing I do will ever be remembered?

—Another Theresa in the Middle

Dear Theresa:

For many bright young people, their first encounter with the world is through books. Histories, stories, plays, even religious texts—all contain stories of the great persons and great deeds of the past, of actions that have moved the fate of the world. It is natural to start thinking you need to measure your own achievements against theirs. But this is nearly impossible and a disservice to yourself, and it can blind you to the realities of the life right in front of you.

I find it telling that you have capitalized "Great Work." As if the only work that would be of significance to you is something on such a grand scale that it is remembered. The question then becomes: Who is it that you want to remember you? Who are you trying to impress? Why are the distant recipients of Great Work more valuable to you than the people who are in your immediate experience?

That's not to say that I'm siding with your husband—who sounds to me like one of those men who value knowledge only as long as they are the sole owners of it. It does sound like you had a different vision of what your marriage could be than he did, and it would behoove you to discuss this with him, regardless of whether you think he'd be receptive to it.

You are working against what society deems as acceptable for a married woman. I would never tell you to give up looking for a way to escape these constraints, either through head-on confrontation or by finding a way to sidestep them. But I would suggest you also begin to consider how you can help to better the lives of the people around you. That may not be a Great Work, but it is good work, and you will see the immediate value in the faces of those you affect.

Dear Aunt Antigone:

I always knew that I wanted to be a writer. I had a plan, and I followed it to the letter. I got straight As in high school, and spent my days studying and reading everything I could get my hands on. Then at college, I was awarded a coveted scholarship, ran the literary magazine, and was secretary of the Honor Board. I wrote poetry, studied the classics, and assumed I'd be accepted to a prestigious graduate school. After that, I thought of perhaps studying in Europe before coming home to settle down as a professor or poet or editor of some kind. My ambition and drive were unstoppable.

This internship was just supposed to be another stop on my march toward my future. One month in New York City, working on Ladies Day *magazine, learning from professionals working in the real world. I'm supposed to be having the time of my life. But I'm not. Instead, I feel exposed.*

One month in New York, and suddenly, all of my achievements seem unimportant, all of my aspirations ludicrous. Suddenly, I am possessed with the knowledge—the certainty—that all of my plans are laughable, that they will never amount to anything. I'm beginning to think that something might be wrong with me.

Part of me wants to hold on, and trust that things will get better once I leave New York. Later this summer, I'm supposed to take a writing course back at Harvard. But another part of me thinks that I should finally listen to my mother and just learn shorthand so I have something to fall back on. What should I do?

—Purely Depressed

Dear Purely:

When we have many successes at an early age, we can start to believe that there are no limits to what we can accomplish. Often our parents and teachers, in seeking to encourage us, actually cause us harm. They tell us that we can do anything we want, that the possibilities are endless. Except that can't actually be true. There are always ends. There are always limits.

The danger is that when you start to discover those limits, when the bad things start to happen—and they will *happen—then there's no way to truly understand or cope with them. The voice in your head begins to ask unsettling questions: "You're supposed to be able to do anything. So if you can't, then whose fault is it? It's got to be yours, right? Something inside of you, some defect, must be the reason. You think the problem isn't whatever happened—you're the problem." Does that logic sound familiar to you? I have a feeling it might.*

But the truth is: bad things happen to everyone. We all make mistakes, we all fail, things that we thought we could count on do not come through, and people we love hurt us. There's nothing we can do to prevent it. What we can *do is not take it all on ourselves, not believe that we are the cause of all our miseries, not internalize it. It's this self-blame that can easily lead to depression and self-isolation.*

You probably don't think you can share this feeling with anyone you really know, but it's imperative that you do. Open up to someone, share your feelings with somebody you trust.

Don't try to hold all this inside, or else you risk it bursting out of you in ways that you can't fathom or control.

—A.A.

Dear Aunt Antigone:

I am caught on the horns of a dilemma of work etiquette and could use an outside opinion. I am a junior solicitor at a respected English law firm. We have a peculiar client: a foreign nobleman interested in acquiring an estate near London. My employer found an ideal location in Purfleet, and I was dispatched to bring our client the deeds of purchase to sign, the plans of the estate, and to render whatever other assistance he might require.

After a long journey with many strange sights, I finally reached the client's castle. He greeted me with all courtesies, but everything here is very strange. He gave me liberty of the castle except for any locked doors, and yet almost every door is locked. There are no servants, though he serves me large meals, from which he never eats a bite. When I have inquired about such peculiar things, he merely replies, "Transylvania is not England."

I have managed to sneak out on a few occasions, and even pushed my way past some of the locked doors. I have seen such strange sights, which I cannot even begin to put into words here. I have seen terrible things that left me somehow transfixed, unable to look away. I am beginning to doubt the count's intentions. However, I am mindful that, when dealing with foreigners, an Englishman's responsibility is understanding, forbearance, and sobriety. Should I endeavour to make an escape? Or should I maintain a stiff upper lip and trust that all will work out as it should?

—Trapped in Transylvania

Dear Trapped:

The advice columnist's job is to get to the underlying, unspoken issues behind the question and help their correspondent look at the problem in different ways so they can decide for themselves. I'm going to make an exception in this case and tell you exactly what you need to do. Leave now. Get out as quickly as you can.

Still reading? Very well, then let's dig into it.

Society functions on implicit and explicit agreements. If someone violates the law, they are sanctioned by civil authorities. If someone violates a norm or a custom, they are ostracized or otherwise punished by social institutions. These systems work because people submit to their rule and allow their lives to be governed by it in exchange for relative peace and safety. But there are always those who look to escape these constraints, who do all they can to subvert, pervert, and twist humanity's laws to their own advantage. We call them "criminals." When they hide their criminal deeds behind great power and prestige, we call them "nobility."

Those who subvert the laws of nature, we label "monsters." The very scope and scale of their transgressions are so out of our ability to comprehend that they become, oddly, attractive. You did not go into detail about the things that you saw on the occasions you escaped your captivity—and make no mistake, it is captivity—but that you found them equally awful and awe-full. And that a part of you wanted to give in to the dark desires that witnessing these depravities stirred in you. If you had given in, then you would not have returned to your room. That you did means that you know on some level how much danger you are in. You can feel it. Only your English propriety, and the strong social inculcation that says you shouldn't bother the powerful, keeps you from taking action.

Forbearance is laudable, up to a point. For you this point has come. So please heed my advice: get away while you still can.

Dear Aunt Antigone:

I am by trade a lawyer and own a small business, for which I employ a number of scriveners. We copy documents for all manner of legal transactions, and I am gratified to say that my reputation for caution and probity has been spoken of by many eminent men, including the great John Jacob Astor himself.

Scrivening is a necessary business, though it can be tedious. As such, I have always found it prudent to be somewhat forgiving of my employees in regards to their individual shortcomings and peccadilloes. But I am now faced with a situation that tests the limits of my forbearance.

Recently, I took on a new scrivener. At first, he was the most dogged, industrious worker I had ever seen, copying everything that I gave to him without any rest or break. I thought myself fortunate and began dreaming of ways I could enlarge my business with such an indefatigable resource at my disposal. But soon, his behavior grew strange. The rate of his copying grew slower and slower, until it dwindled to almost nothing. And most peculiar of all, whenever I would make a request of him for some such documents or copy, he began to give the same response, "I would prefer not to."

No amount of inquiry or pressure has been able to induce him to resume his former work, even at a modicum of its once robust pace. He now sits like a statue, immovable, taking up space in my office, not producing anything, and causing an uproar among the other scriveners. He is unfailingly polite and almost apologetic, as if he is helpless, as if all of this is out of his control, and yet he will not rouse himself to do anything. I would be well within my rights to simply fire him. To call the constables and have him taken to the Tombs. And yet, his countenance is so sad and pitiable, I cannot bring myself to do so.

I would appreciate your suggestions for how to motivate him to return to his work or get him to quit my office completely.

—A Master in Chancery

Dear Master:

It would seem that your course of action is obvious. You have an employee who refuses to perform the function for which you have hired him, therefore you are well within your rights to dismiss him and remove him from your premises. And while this mysterious scrivener's behavior seems inexplicable, I'm much more interested in your reactions.

Why, exactly, do you think you are reluctant to call the constables? You describe his "sad and pitiable" countenance—why should it be that his sadness matters to you more than the masses of the pitiable that you likely pass on your way to and from your office? Is it because you are forced to see it every day, all day long, and cannot hide from it?

I'm sorry that I don't have answers for you, only more questions. But your practical question seems to mask a deeper issue—as a lawyer, you deal with contracts, rules, and procedures. At the moment, you are faced with someone who is refusing to follow those rules, and it unsettles you. Oh, there are always people who stand up to defy the law—I myself have been known to do that on occasion. Even when one loudly denounces or attacks the established rules, it usually comes from a place rooted in the recognition of those rules.

But your troublesome employee is not protesting against your business, he's not damning you for corruption or working against your interest. He is simply, passively, refusing to be a part of it. It's your scrivener's politeness amidst his helplessness that you find so disconcerting. I submit that you won't feel comfortable getting rid of him until you can place his resistance into some neatly labeled box and decide under which heading it can be filed away.

Such logical, literal-mindedness is to be expected from one in the law profession. That you find this so unsettling would indicate that you've glimpsed a part of the world that such law, order, and logic cannot explain.

As much as we sometimes wish it were otherwise, law and reason have their limits. How you learn to live with that unsettling fact will determine how you decide your scrivener's fate.

Chapter 7

MONEY MATTERS

As one might expect, most of the letters I receive are about problems of love and romantic relationships. But I get almost as many that deal with questions about money. And as you'd also expect, these issues are almost never really about money itself. Instead, they're about value, opportunity, and the place where one fits in society. So, money questions really are relationship questions after all.

Even if you were born into a wealthy family, it seems that there is never enough money to go around. Or if there is, it always provokes some kind of battle over who gets access to wealth, who is denied, and who is empowered to make those decisions.

But money is just a metaphor; it's the way we measure our individual standing against the rest of the world. It's a tool, an emblem, a stand-in, and a validation all in one. But money isn't the only marker of value. It's easy to lose sight of that. When we do, the losses we incur are immeasurable.

Dear Aunt Antigone:

There is nothing more humiliating than looking poor while among the rich, which is a burden I suffer daily. I have no gowns, I have no jewels, and so I have stopped showing my face to rich friends, as their condescension fills me with rage. I am just as deserving as they of a fine, luxurious life, but because of a slip of fate, I was born to an inconsequential family and made to marry a lowly clerk.

Recently somehow, my husband was able to get an invitation to a ball at the Ministry. I panicked! I had nothing remotely suitable to wear and not until I sobbed would my husband agree to give me four hundred francs to buy a dress. But even then, I had no jewelry. How could I dare to make an appearance without wearing at least one jewel? Swallowing my embarrassment, I asked a wealthy friend if she would lend me something for the night. I expected her to laugh in my face and throw me out, as I might have done had I been in her position. But to my shock, she gave me a free hand to choose anything she owned. And the moment she opened the box, I knew what I saw was perfect—the most exquisite diamond necklace I'd ever laid eyes upon.

With that necklace, my appearance at the ball was a triumph. I did not lack for dance partners or conversation. I overheard people I did not know commenting on my beauty. I even caught the notice of the minister himself. It was one of the most thrilling nights of my life, and on the cab ride home I thought that nothing could ever rob me of the evening's memory. How wrong I was.

When we got home, I discovered the necklace had gone missing. I sent my husband out to track down the cab and to retrace our steps, but he could not find it. I searched and searched but came up empty. It was gone.

Now, I am frozen with panic. Do I confess to my friend that I lost her gorgeous necklace, and thus humiliate myself even further, proving for all time that I do not belong in the society of the wealthy and beautiful? Or do I try to replace it, even though the cost will impoverish my husband and me for years to come?

—Bare-Necked and Abashed

Dear Abashed:

What an unfortunate turn of events! It seems so unfair, after having such a wonderful, rare experience at the ball to only have the memory snatched away by losing your friend's necklace. I do not doubt how bad you feel in this moment. However, I do find it telling that you don't actually seem too concerned about your friend's feelings. It was her possession you lost. She could feel hurt, angered, or betrayed. She could be wrathful, disappointed, unforgiving. But none of that seems to matter to you as much as your own potential loss of status.

You express fear about both potential humiliation and anxiety about fitting in among the rich. This is a dangerous place from which to make decisions. Desperation can lead to rash choices and to an urge to avoid short-term pain that ends up costing you more in the long run. But if you have to choose between incurring a great cost or opening yourself up to more humiliation, which one would you choose? Or, more precisely, which one is more intolerable to you? Which one could you not live with?

Confession or restitution—you've laid out these two options as an either/or choice. Has it occurred to you that a third option would be to do both: to confess to your friend and *offer restitution? I am not surprised that it hasn't, but I would strongly advise you to consider it. Whatever humiliation you fear might be leavened by forthrightness and leave room for your friend to show her own generosity. But that would require honesty, and a willingness to risk being humiliated, which so terrifies you. Can you put a price on that?*

Dear Aunt Antigone:

They say great men are justified in committing crimes if it leads to the creation of a better future. Lycurgus, Solon, Mahomet, Napoleon, and so on were all without exception criminals, but their crimes created better worlds. I do not mean to say that I am a Napoleon. I am merely a poor student. Ex-student, really. I subsist on what translation work I can find, do a small amount of writing, and spend my days avoiding both my landlady and the drunks of St. Petersburg. But who is to say what I might become were I to undertake some kind of extreme action that bettered society?

There is a pawnbroker of my acquaintance, a loathsome creature who preys on the poor, cheats them out of what little they have, and even beats her poor sister. Such riches, in the middle of awful poverty; she hoards her wealth more than the tsar himself. How much good could be done with that money, if it were taken from her and used to improve the lot of the poor? What is the value of one underserving old person's life against hundreds, thousands of others?

A strange idea keeps pecking at my brain like a chicken in the egg. Could not one tiny crime be wiped out if the result were thousands of good deeds?

—A Divided Mind

Dear Divided:

Isn't logic a wonderful thing? We believe that we are all logical thinkers, rational beings with the ability to look at the world around us, make sober, informed judgments, and choose a course of action accordingly. In this ideal, cause leads to effect. Premise leads to conclusion. Everything works the way that it should. But open your eyes and take a good look around and you'll see that none of that is really true. We are creatures of irrationality, of strange ideas and stranger desires.

It might be true that taking the wealth of this one woman would allow you to do good for many more people. Are you willing to be the one that makes that decision on behalf of society? Are you willing to pay the price for it? You're certainly trying to talk yourself into it. You have marshaled a few logical arguments, and I'd bet that if pressed you could come up with dozens more. I imagine that these lines of thought buzz around in your head, bolstering your courage, pushing you forward. You're probably seeing signs everywhere that are telling you to go forward with it. Are you writing to me because you want another confirmation that your contemplated crime is justified, or are you hoping for a clear signal to stop? I'm not going to take on that responsibility for you. You must choose for yourself, the same way everyone else does, every day.

I'll simply ask you to consider if the difference between your so-called Napoleons and common criminals is less related to their relative "greatness," and more about whether or not they got caught. Napoleon had an army to defend him. What do you have?

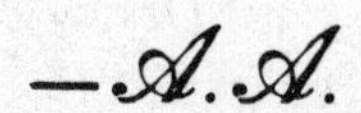

Dear Aunt Antigone:

I've been a total fool. I often find myself at the mercy of a passion for gambling on bridge games, and it has gotten me in considerable trouble. But that's nothing compared to my current predicament. An acquaintance introduced me to the idea of speculating in the stock market, and I allowed him to do so on my behalf. At first, it seemed like free money! And it was an easy way to keep up with all of my expenses.

Then I found out that he'd been telling others about my investments. Society people were talking about us in quite an indiscreet manner, making insinuations, which I did my best to ignore. Soon, my acquaintance began behaving with disagreeable familiarity toward me in public, as if he felt entitled to some shadowy claim over me. He went so far as to trick me into being alone with him in his apartment, inviting me under the pretense of visiting his wife when he knew that she had not come down from Bellomont. While I was trapped alone with him, he made it clear that he expected repayment—and not in money. It was all I could do to escape.

It is now painfully clear to me the manner in which I am spoken about behind my back. If there is any hope of salvaging my standing, I must pay back all of the money that he gave to me. My aunt could certainly bail me out, but the idea of laying myself open for her scorn is intolerable. I could try my luck again at the card table, but I see no indication that my fortunes would be any different than before. I suppose I could just marry a rich man, but all efforts in that direction have so far failed. Otherwise, I am at a loss, and I fear that all of New York society will make me a pariah.

How does one make a large sum of money quickly without having to sell a part of themselves?

—Mirthless in Manhattan

Dear Mirthless:

That your "friend" expected recompense in-kind for his investment advice does not shock me. Many men, and many societies, turn everything into a commodity: stocks, bonds, natural resources, affections, bodies, futures. When you have an abundance of these commodities, the world can seem limitless. Anything can happen! Anything is possible! It doesn't even take losing them to throw the good times into jeopardy. All it requires is the threat, the mere possibility that you might end up with less. Especially when you can see others with so much more.

Let's approach your problem from an economic viewpoint. You have something you wish to purchase: your standing in society. What do you have to sell in order to make that exchange? Or, more precisely, what are you willing to sell? It has to be something—your virtue, your marriage prospects, your self-respect in the face of your aunt's disapproval. Do you have anything else? It may not seem like you have much, but you do have more than many. Most people have to sell their time, their labor, their lives, in order to get a little bit of the money they need. Maybe you're getting off easy?

But the money always has to come from somewhere, doesn't

it? You'll need to make some difficult choices about what you really want, what you'll accept, and what you'll exchange in return.

Dear Aunt Antigone:

Throughout all of Venice I am despised, spit upon, insulted. And yet, when the Christians have need of me, they come to me with all their politeness, all their courtesies, as if I cannot remember today what they said of me last Wednesday. These Christians preach love and fairness and friendship when it suits them, but the moment I advance my own cause, I am met with nothing but oppression, torment, and villainy.

One such of these merchants have I entered into a contract with. I have lent him thousands of ducats, bonded, notarized, and agreed to under all of the city's laws. This merchant has often tormented me, disgraced me, laughed at my misfortunes. He and his brothers have stopped at nothing to make sure that my brethren and I are made to feel like aliens in our own home. As it happens, this merchant has defaulted on his bond, and placed me in a position to demand recompense. The terms of our agreement are not for the standard coinage, but for a bloodier collateral. Not thinking my word is worth anything, he asks me to forgo my due. But I cannot forget his insults.

Now he contrives to have the duke intercede on his behalf, and thus to rob me of my deserts. They offer to make me whole, to replenish my coffers, to repay me at a premium. All that it requires of me is to be merciful and forgo the blood debt. But why should I? Have they been merciful to me? No. Am I treating them with the same kindness that they show to me? Yes.

Am I wrong to insist on what is lawfully mine? If I give in to them, will my name forever be demeaned as one who can be used without consequence? May I not choose my principles over my interest?

—An Honest Moneylender

Dear Moneylender:

While you try to gloss it over, I can't help but pick out the reference to "bloodier collateral." You offer no details, but I can only assume that it refers to something that the other party to the contract is loath to part with. One might wonder why he offered it in the first place, but I recognize that often when we are pressed with the exigencies of need, we agree to things that we later regret. Have you never made an arrangement which you wish you could have taken back? Said things in harsh surety that later you wish had been delivered with more sweetness?

Nevertheless, you are certainly legally entitled to receive your due. The fact that a higher authority has been brought into the matter should be worrisome to you. You talk at length about how you feel the city's Christians treat your people—so do you expect that the ruler of that city will deal with you any differently? Is he a neutral arbiter? Or would you be better off cutting your losses and accepting their counteroffer?

But let's be honest, it's not about the money at all, is it? You talk about contracts, payments, fair recompense, but underneath it all, what you're really asking about is revenge. Is it permissible to take revenge on someone who has wronged you? I could make a moral case to you about turning the other cheek or about how revenge belongs to the heavens. But you know all of those arguments. So let's talk practicalities.

You seem to be well within your rights to exact your revenge. Just know that doing so will often only lead to a reciprocal next act of revenge, which begets another, and another, and soon the whole affair can easily spiral out of control. Resentments build on top of each other until nobody can remember the original sin. This is usually the thing that keeps us from enacting revenge, even when it is justified. The bill is too steep. But sometimes, there are so many resentments that the thought of accepting just one more is intolerable. That's when the prospect of starting a war seems to be worth it.

Is your need for revenge so strong that you are willing to bear the subsequent costs it will incur, in money, in blood, and in myriad unforeseen consequences? Answer that, and you'll know what to do.

Dear Aunt Antigone:

I am so sorely vexed, and I know not where else to turn. My husband is a gentleman with two thousand a year. I thought marrying into the gentry meant that I'd never have to worry about fortune ever again. Oh, how wrong I was! Five daughters I have, and none of them settled. Because our estate is entailed and my husband has no male heirs, upon his death it will go to a distant cousin, and he may very well throw us all out on our ears! And my uncompassionate husband refuses to see the danger that looms for us all. Mr. B just mocks me and hides in his study, oblivious to all our problems and worries. But it's people like me with a nervous condition who are always mindful of what terrible calamities the future might bring. Just thinking about it sends me into a fit.

But a stroke of good fortune has befallen us. A very wealthy gentleman has recently taken up at a great estate not three miles away.. By all accounts he gets four or five thousand a year! If my oldest could but catch his eye, then all of our problems would be solved. But I am in a quandary. There is to be a ball, and to make her and her sisters presentable will come at a considerable cost. In the past, I would not hesitate to incur the expense. But heaven help me, the unthinkable is becoming thinkable! I wonder if we should instead save as much as we can against that terrible future day when we lose everything?

—Cruelly Used

Dear Cruelly:

Saving for the future is never a bad idea. Some would tell you to assume the worst, take the most prudent path available, and start planning for the day when you will lose it all. But I don't get the sense that you are one to sit around and wait for fortune to have its way with you. Sometimes you have to invest in yourself, even if your resources are dwindling. Playing it safe is not always the best option.

More troubling is your husband's indifference to the problem. You say he retreats to his study to avoid his share of shouldering the burden. Is there some other way you could make him listen to your worries? He may be a gentleman, but he is also a father and a husband, and if he is neglecting his responsibilities in those areas you are well within your rights to tell him that.

I would, however, caution you against pushing your daughters too hard. Cast your mind back to when you were their age. Did you have relatives telling you what you should do? Did you listen to them? And though you are in a precarious position, is it more important that they marry someone—anyone—than it is that they choose husbands of character? Think about what message you are imparting to them. Does this newly arrived gentleman have any say in the matter? Have you even made his acquaintance?

Not everything will need to be decided at this one ball. Marriage, as you well know, is a long game. Husband your resources accordingly, but do not be afraid to act boldly when necessary.

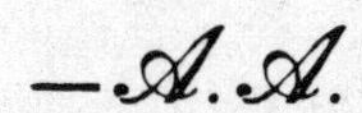

Dear Aunt Antigone:

I have a long memory. There was a man who thwarted me, many years ago, and I swore I would see my revenge. But I have grown old. I have settled down from my former wanderings, I have married, and I have started a good, respectable business. I have, in short, become comfortable. Thoughts of my revenge began to subside when replaced by my present responsibilities and ease.

But then I found him. Not the man who wronged me—he is long dead. But one who knows his secrets, who knows where to dig them up. This second man died of fright, rather than face me, and his maps went into the hands of landsmen, inexperienced and easy to manipulate—why, they have even approached me to outfit their expedition. The good vessel Hispaniola *departs soon, and all it would take is a word from me and I will be on my way toward the treasure that should have always been mine.*

I'm old. My stump hurts. I have grown comfortable here at the inn, and in bed with my wife. I do not need to go a-sea again. I don't need the money. But I want it. I dream of it.

I swore to have my revenge, and now it is at hand. But have I grown out of needing it? Should I just forget the treasure and stay home?

—The Legless Quartermaster

Dear Quartermaster:

You say that you don't need the money. But some debts are measured in other ways. The hurts of our past can stay with us for longer than we ever imagined. Physical injuries heal, and we can learn to survive without all of the abilities we had when we were younger. But mental injuries can last a lot longer. And they can recur when you least expect them.

Which way tips the balance, when on one side sits this treasure and on the other rests your wife, your home, your comfort in old age? If you did not pursue it, would you be able to sleep at night? How much is that sleep worth to you? Will you continue to dream of the money, or will that vision eventually fade? As you say, you don't really need the money. But can a price even be put on revenge?

Recognize that there are many different kinds of treasures. What good will it do if you pursue one, only to lose another of greater value? Though for certain persons, the prospect of having it all is too alluring to resist. Is that you?

Most importantly, what does your wife think? She is your first mate, your constant partner. Shouldn't she have a say in what you decide?

Dear Aunt Antigone:

My repeated requests to be left alone continue to be ignored by prattling knaves who profess to have my best interest at heart, yet I know they only desire to take what I have worked hard to earn. I have just chased two such men from my premises, two so-called Christians demanding some of my hard-earned money for the benefit of the poor. *What do we have the workhouses for? I asked them. The prisons? Do not my taxes support these institutions? Why should I pay one penny more for the benefit of people who do not produce anything for society? Better they die off and reduce the surplus population.*

All manner of man around me moan and palaver about Christmas. But Christmas is nothing to me but a day in which I am thwarted from my business, when all the shops are closed, when my clerk expects a day of liberty and still to be paid. Why am I the only one to see how mad this is?

It is enough for a man to understand his own business, and not to interfere with that of others. Mine occupies me constantly. What will it take for others to mind theirs and leave me out of it?

—Hater of Humbug

Dear Humbug:

Because the money is yours, you are right, you should not be impelled to part with it by anyone. Even if they think it's for a good reason. After all, you earned that money. It is the fruit of your hard-fought labors, isn't it?

But then ask yourself: All of this money that is yours, what is it for? Do you count it up, pore over ledgers, tally and retally the sums? Do the numbers keep you warm? Do your ledgers care for you when you are sick? Does your coin love you?

Ask yourself another question: Who have you taken this money from? What are their conditions? From whom will your next monies come? Do you expect that one day you will be able to gather up all the money in the world for yourself? You want other people to leave you alone and mind their own business. But you are part of a society. You cannot remove yourself from it, no more than you could separate one part of your body—the heart?—from the rest of the whole.

Christmas comes once a year. What if, on that one day, you tried gifting others with a generosity of spirit instead of walling yourself off from everyone else. Could you do that for one day? If so, you might discover that giving is a conduit to receiving back more—not just money but also connection, esteem, love.

Or you can go about using your coin to shield you from all that society, all those people. If so, then eventually, they will all leave you to your own, final business.

Dear Aunt Antigone:

I married Charles when I was very young. At the time, all I knew of the world was what I read in books. For a while I was happy with him. But that all began to change after the ball at La Vaubyessard. There for the first time, I saw for myself what it meant to have a rich life. With Charles, my fate was to be the poor wife of a village doctor. But I began to dream of more.

Since then I have tried to give myself the life I deserve, mostly through purchasing beautiful, fine luxuries. When I started, it was a mere occasional indulgence, but now I am unable to stop. Presently, I find that I am in tremendous debt and I do not know where to turn. Monsieur L______ holds so many bills. Recently, I had a visit from the bailiff. I have had to sell off many of my nice things in order to pay a fraction of what I owe. But it's not nearly enough.

Whenever I sit down to do the calculations, the sums are so exorbitant as to defy belief. How could it get to be this much? I get so bewildered that I must stop thinking about it altogether lest my old nervous condition reassert itself. I have banished Charles to the second floor. I stay up all night, reading, trying to lose myself in fantasies of richer lives. But in the morning, I am still only me.

There are men who have loved me in the past. Perhaps I could go to them and beg them to lend me the money I need. But if they will not help me, I do not know what else I will do. Have I ruined everything? Is there to be any escape for me?

—Madame Endetté

Dear Endetté:

When debts spiral, it can be murderous to try to get them under control. While I cannot advise you on particular solutions—for that, you'd need a financial adviser, dear—I can perhaps direct your attention to a flaw in your thinking that may have contributed to your predicament: an overreliance on belief.

You say that you "deserved" to have a richer life? Why? Why you and not someone else? Oh, I know the real answer—we all like to have nice things, we all have ambitions and hopes for the future and for bettering our situation. But by draping this natural drive in the cloak of "deserving," you have made it too dear, created a situation where any tiny evidence of a lack of finery, of riches, of advancement, becomes intolerable. You also wrote that when you try to do the calculations of all your debts, the totals are so high as to "defy belief" and your only remedy is to give up examining the problem, which only serves to exacerbate it. You cannot solve what you ignore.

The outcome of all this is that you are isolated, alone, on the verge of illness, and considering desperate measures to escape the consequences of your actions. Which leads to a third belief that you may not know that you hold: the conviction that the consequences of your mistakes are too much to bear and that you lack the strength to endure them. What would happen if you were totally honest with your husband about all your transgressions? What would happen if you welcomed the bailiff? Would you be censured? Would you be jailed? Would you be made an outcast? Perhaps all of these things would come to pass.

But to me, it sounds like you are already jailed, already censured, already casting yourself out. How much worse would it be if you were to accept your fate instead of looking for more and more desperate ways to avoid it? Might you discover that you are stronger than you think?

Chapter 8

COMMUNITY *and* SOCIETY

As men and women of the world, we are all part of a community, a society, a culture. Each of these particular groups subscribes to their own laws and customs, which in turn give rise to particular biases, internal conflicts, and blind spots. None of us solely belong to ourselves. We each have to relate to the world around us, fit ourselves into our communities, choose which customs to obey and which to flout. However, we can often be so focused on the personal nature of our problems that we cannot see how they arise from our environment. Or the reverse is true, and we conflate social problems into personal ones. And sometimes, there is no real difference between the two. Our individual choices can affect our community, and the strictures that our society places on us can profoundly change our personal lives.

Our choices can also bring us into conflict with our family and loved ones. I loved my sister with all my heart, and in my younger days, I believed that nothing could ever tear us apart. Nevertheless, when we faced the greatest challenge of our lives, we found ourselves on opposite sides from each other. She chose to follow the law, while I defied it in the name of ancient customs. We both paid for our choices.

So, although we are each one small part of a larger whole, ultimately, we're each answerable to our own individual conscience. Navigating between the two is not a simple task.

Dear Aunt Antigone:

I live among Puritans. They are judgmental and unforgiving. I am considered a pariah for a transgression that I committed long ago, something for which I have been punished, accepted the consequences, and if I am honest, do not regret. I only regret the consequences for my daughter.

We now live on the outskirts of the town near the dark forest. The good people of Massachusetts Bay do not want us dwelling any closer, not with the reminder of my act so visible on my chest. And yet, though I am despised, it does not keep those same upstanding citizens from employing me as a seamstress. My morals may be suspect, but my stitches are not, and I do fine work for all the most notable, including the governor. I even perform charitable works for the poor and downtrodden, although they scorn me just as much as the rich do—if not more.

I could leave. I could take my daughter, return to England or go anywhere else, change my name, and start again without this visible sign of sin upon me. In spite of all this, I stay, and I'm not entirely sure why. I don't think these good people will ever forgive me, for I am forever tainted in their eyes. So why do I continue to subject myself to their derision? How can I ever prove to them that I am not the sinful creature they think I am?

—A Living Sermon

Dear Sermon:

You say that you've been punished, and you have accepted your punishment. Still, your neighbors treat you as an outcast. In some ways, this is understandable. No society I have knowledge of has yet to invent a method of dispensing law that is entirely fair and equitable. Therefore, we all, to some extent, rely on the decisions of those we invest with authority, and use those decisions to divide the world into good and bad, righteous and corrupt, acceptable and shunned. And while much talk is given to concepts of forgiveness and rehabilitation, once you're branded a criminal it's hard to escape the label.

But people are not fixed entities. We change, and so does society. So do morals and needs. Your neighbors seem to have no problem with situational ethics, allowing themselves to make use of your skills when they feel like it, but always reminding you of your place while they do it. I am not surprised that you have a desire to leave. And yet you don't listen to that desire.

Do you want to prove to them that they are wrong about you? What will that gain you if you do prove that? Is that esteem worth the suffering you put yourself through—not to mention what your daughter must also face? Besides, don't you have that esteem already, every time one of them wears one of your garments? Their hypocrisy is your validation. So why isn't that enough?

Is there something else keeping you there? Something you

need to prove to yourself? You may not be in a position to share the facts of that with anybody else, but at least you should be clear about it with yourself—otherwise you'll never find peace.

—*A.A.*

Dear Aunt Antigone:

I am resting in the hospital after being struck by a car—how ironic!—and so have nothing to do but think. How things have changed. When I was a boy, my family was the richest in town. The buildings, the streets, even the opera house bore our magnificent name. I thought it was the natural way of things and would always be.

I was conceited, cruel, and arrogant. I thought I was entitled to whatever I wanted, without having to work for it. The people in town hated me and wished that one day I would get my comeuppance. I laughed in their faces. I was so spoiled, especially by my long-suffering mother. I made her pay for it most of all. I made her choose between me and the man she loved, knowing she could never say no to me.

Now, mother is dead. The major too. They've all died or left. Only my aunt and I remain. She has her heart set on living in a boarding house with some of her old cronies, and I don't know how I am going to afford it. The family fortune is gone, squandered through bad investments. The buildings and the streets all have different names now. It's like we've been erased. They all wished for me to get my comeuppance, and now it seems I've gotten it.

Is my fate sealed by the mistakes of my youth? Is it too late for me to make something different or better of my life?

—Rides Down Everything

Dear Rides:

I sympathize with what you're going through. I know what it's like to be brought up to believe that you are important and special, only to have the world rip away everything you know. Call it the will of the gods or call it progress, nothing is constant except change.

But while you have felt the brunt of that, it is also cause for you to have hope. As the world can always change, so can you. It's never too late. In some ways, you've already done the hard work. Your illusions have been already destroyed. You can no longer live the way you once did, be the person you once were.

You now have the opportunity to become a totally different person, without the luxurious trap of falling back on old habits. You get to decide who that person is, and how they fit into the world. If the old version of you was self-centered, cruel, and conceited, then what would it feel like if you became generous, responsible, and humble? When you encounter people who knew you during your childhood, what might happen if you met them with these new qualities? Might you find that the people who once hated you could grow to love you? Might you redeem yourself, and find a new way forward?

Can you use your comeuppance to lift your own self up too?

Dear Aunt Antigone:

Some may call me sheltered, but I have read many books, and from them I believe that I know more about how the world works than some might think. When one sees an injustice, one is duty bound to report it to the rightful authorities. Society depends on justice for the wicked.

I was recently invited to visit with friends. It's exactly the sort of event that in a book would mark the beginning of a heroine's adventure—a stay at a stately home, Gothic, foreboding, and full of secrets. General T. and his family have been nothing but gracious. I began to wonder if perhaps what I've read in my books had misled me. But then! I learned of something quite suspicious. There are rooms in the home that no one is permitted to set foot in. It's like something out of an Ann Radcliffe novel! What secrets might be concealed within?

The rooms belonged to the general's late wife, who died several years ago. And upon further acquaintance, the general seems to me to be a strange man. I thought at first that perhaps he had murdered her. But then a more distressing and likely scenario occurred to me—what if she is still alive and imprisoned in those rooms?! I have taken it upon myself to spy on the general and learn what he is really up to. Perhaps in the night he will sneak down to the locked room to visit his imprisoned wife or to perform some other dark and daring scheme.

In my novels, the villain always does something to bring about their own demise. So I have sworn to stay alert so I may discover the truth. But as of now, all I have are my suspicions.

I so wish to do the good and right thing. Should I alert someone in authority now before the general does something worse? Or do I need to collect more proof first, even though it may put me in the path of danger?

—*Conscientiously Gothic*

Dear Gothic:

Many people would dismiss your speculation out of hand. I don't want to be so hasty—in my experience there are people in the world capable of doing such dark and heinous things as you describe. And yet . . .

I must caution you that if you wish to make a compelling case for such nefarious doings on the part of this general, you'll need a lot more concrete evidence. The law does well with documents, with eyewitnesses, with testimony. But all you have is speculation.

You seem to have more knowledge of the world through reading about it than you do with direct experience. This is not something to be ashamed of, for reading can be a wonderful way to experience parts of life you do not have direct access to. And even the most well-traveled person can never see everything.

But you must remember that when you read a story, you are consuming something that has been constructed with the aim of holding your attention, with propelling your thoughts along a certain track. Heroines in Gothic novels are all of a certain type, and they all take similar journeys, but ultimately these tales are meant to entertain you. They are not meant as models for behavior or as pictures of the way the world works. Reality is much messier. It may seem to you that the disorder and absence of a clear narrative structure make the real world less compelling than one of your books. But I can promise you that it actually makes it infinitely more interesting.

So, snoop through the house if you must. But be prepared to discover that the dark Gothic secrets that you perceive are nothing but fragments of a real person's story, a story that you have not heard a full account of. And know that you will need to hear that full story before you can draw any real conclusions.

Dear Aunt Antigone:

When I was a young man, I was naive and trusting. I believed in honor. Then the world demonstrated to me how wrong I was. Betrayal at the hands of those who I thought were my friends taught me to hate. Fourteen years of imprisonment in the Château d'If taught me so much more and filled me with a longing for retribution. After I finally made my escape, I swore to spend my life getting revenge on those who wronged me. Men of faith may say that what I am doing is immoral, and that vengeance belongs only to God. But I say they are wrong. I say that a world that would allow an innocent man to suffer as I have suffered has given up all rights to tell me how to behave.

Now, I am enacting my revenge. I feel no remorse, I feel no doubt. In fact, I feel nothing. I would have counted on justice bringing feelings of triumph and vindication, but apart from a certain grim satisfaction that my plans work as expected, nothing brings me joy. All I feel is numbness.

If a permanent loss of happiness is the price I need to pay for my vengeance, I will gladly pay it a thousand times over. But must the two be mutually exclusive?

—Unaccounted For

Dear Unaccounted:

If society functioned as it should, justice would take the place of vengeance. But when society fails, sometimes revenge is all you have left. Legion are those who take up the cause of vengeance with the same moral determination that you profess. Most of them end up causing suffering for other innocents, and so the cycle of injustice continues. I'm not saying that you will go down the same road. I am merely pointing out that, in your suffering, you have allowed yourself to believe a story in which your pain, your hurt, your injustices, outweigh any other concerns.

I do think, however, that your lack of feeling any joy from your revenge is a positive sign, as strange as that might seem to you. If you were enjoying it more, you might soon find yourself needing to hurt people to feel anything, regardless of whether they have wronged you or not. This is how sadists are made.

The numbness that so troubles you is, in fact, a sign of hope. It's an effective defense mechanism. Our bodies invoke it when the pain of feeling is too much for us to handle. But numbness can't last forever. Sooner or later, the feelings must be felt.

You've decided it's better to feel nothing rather than feel pain, and that you'll only be allowed to feel again after you have achieved your revenge. But I think those beliefs are wrong. In fact, they're exactly what stands in your way. I contend that you're afraid that if you allow yourself to feel joy again, if you open your heart to someone, then it might blunt your drive for vengeance. Perhaps it might. Perhaps it might not. But you're only going to find out if you try.

Dear Aunt Antigone:

Someone with whom I'm quite well acquainted wrote to you recently about finding a balance between his work and his true inner life. How naive he was. You managed to see through him, which is why I am writing to you now.

My "friend," as you surmised and cautioned him against, gave in to his inner temptations, for which I am grateful, as it has finally allowed me to achieve my full expression. How tiresome it's been, looking at the world through his eyes for so long yet unable to exert my will on it. Poor Doctor Harry believes his drugs keep him in control of us. But he's starting to learn that he's wrong about that too. And as much as he beats his breast and deplores my crimes and my violence, in his secret heart he enjoys them as much as I do.

The plain truth is that I am more suited to this world than he is. His delicacies, his scruples, his morals, his notion of polite London society—they're all fictions. This is a nasty and brutish world. As I am a nasty brute, I belong here more than he ever did. Having finally been liberated, I have no intention of going back inside my cage.

However, as much as he would like to portray me as a mindless animal, I'm not unreasonable. I am open to some agreement where we could share control. Unfortunately for him, the doctor does not agree, and he is taking steps that will ensure both of us are made to suffer. But if I am not permitted my liberty, I will destroy us both.

I only want to have the chance to live and pursue my own happiness. Don't I have that right?

—Hiding in Plain Sight

Dear Hiding:

All creatures should have the right to live and to coexist— peacefully *coexist—with others. This is an ethical cornerstone of many societies, and as close to a universal good as it may be possible to articulate. And yet no philosophy is wholly perfect, and malefactors of all kinds will patiently search for the logical loopholes to justify their crimes. Which is exactly what you are trying to do. But I'm not going to help you in that endeavor.*

The rhetoric you're employing is called the "fallacy of tolerance"—wherein someone engaging in intolerant behavior, when faced with censure, cries that they are themselves the victim of intolerance. Because tolerance is considered a social good, often this charge is enough to make someone withdraw their accusation, and the result is that the original perpetrator continues their intolerable behavior unchecked.

You admit to being a violent criminal. This is intolerable behavior. Some pleasures are indefensible, and yours fall into that category. I do not think you will care to hear the message, but if perchance your "friend" reads this, he should know that balance cannot be found through coexistence with evil. Sometimes, that balance can be found only through self-sacrifice.

Dear Aunt Antigone:

I find myself in the midst of a row over the Social Question about how we of wealth can best assist the poor and lower classes. My sister has made the acquaintance of a young clerk who worked at an insurance company. My new fiancé is a man of business (where my sister and I are more attuned to the arts and intellectual concerns), and when Henry heard the name of this clerk's employer, he told us that the company was in a bad way. My sister relayed the information, and Mr. Bast promptly found employment elsewhere at either reduced or greatly reduced circumstance—the exact amount of the reduction is a matter of debate.

But now, Henry has revised his assessment of the insurance company's prospects. My sister flew into a rage, blaming him for making her friend suffer when there was no need. For his part, Henry disclaims any responsibility. To his mind, business is business, any attempt to advance equality is doomed to failure.

I find myself caught in the middle, but I am afraid that between his stubbornness and her passion there may be no bridge to build toward peace. Is there some way I can reconcile them?

—Trying to Connect

Dear Trying:

As our lives are constantly turning, we all tend to prioritize the problems right in front of us, the immediate discomforts, the conflicts with those whom we know, for those tend to be the most pressing. The larger problems are so vast, so omnipresent, that they seem impossible to solve.

It seems that you find yourself in the middle of an issue that is both personal and concerned with the greater "Social Question," as you call it, and you seek to find a compromise, a way for all parties to be able to coexist peacefully. This is a laudable goal.

Compromise is good. Compromise is essential. Without compromise, we would all be at war, eternally, with everyone. But compromise can't always solve every problem. For one thing, compromise is hard. *It means that nobody gets everything they want, and nobody is completely happy. This in turn builds resentment and makes subsequent compromises more difficult. But what if there is no common ground? What if these two ideas are irreconcilable? What if there is no way to connect?*

Of course, it is to be hoped that your fiancé and your sister can find common ground. I wonder if the poor clerk can be fitted somewhere into such an agreement, or if he will remain an afterthought in this situation.

The most powerful thing about wealth is that it allows you choice. That is, it allows you multiple opportunities to make choices. But how many choices does that clerk have? What are the costs of his choosing wrongly? You may not be able to solve the entire "Social Question," but you might be able to help get him another chance. And if that doesn't exactly promote the peace you're looking for in your household, it may help you find peace within yourself.

Dear Aunt Antigone:

There is right, and there is wrong. Justice is found in the law. Honor and villainy are opposites. Authority and anarchy cannot coexist. Men must be punished for their sins, for breaking the law, even if it is for something as seemingly "small" as stealing a loaf of bread. Wrongdoings must have consequences. This I have always believed, and I have built the entirety of my life on these principles. It was right and good, of this I was sure. But recently, I have had an experience that fills me with confusion.

*There is a man whom I know—*I know*—to be a pure villain, a crafty criminal of unrepentant malice who would commit any offense to escape justice. And yet, I was witness to this man committing an act of mercy that I would not have thought possible for one such as him. Indeed, I must confess that I was a recipient of this mercy.*

If such a terrible man can perform such an act, does this mean that I am wrong, have been wrong for my whole life? Can villainy become honor? Is there no division between right and wrong? Are all the rules on which society is constructed mere fictions?

I do not know how to make sense of this. Is it possible that morality and justice can be different from each other? And if it is possible, then how can I pursue one at the expense of the other?

—Inspecting My Motives

Dear Inspecting:

Oh my dear, you have had a nasty shock. You may not be able to see this now, but you have been given a gift. Most of us live our lives looking only at what is right in front of us. We ceaselessly pursue the next need, the next desire, and we concoct some story to justify it. We invent words and ideas and philosophies to explain why the world behaves as it does, and why we do what we do. We preach and promulgate these philosophies to the world, and declare our society defined by them. In doing so, we lose touch with the original human needs that drove the process.

This man whom you regard as a villain has done something that fills you with doubt about everything you believe. But he would not be able to do this if something in your beliefs wasn't inherently unstable. It's worth looking at where your beliefs came from, and the needs that drove you to create them, to find that point of incongruence. You may be too emotionally raw to do this exploration on you own, so let me give you a place to start.

The worldview you've expressed is quite rigid. You value categorizations and definitions: things are either right or wrong, moral or immoral, honorable or villainous. But any honest assessment of humanity will show that each of us is capable of both infinite kindness and infinite cruelty. That you have clung to such firm distinctions tells me that at one point in your life, you felt at the mercy of a world that was out of control, unendurable, and nonsensical. If that is true, then it makes sense that you created this black-and-white system of morality and meaning for yourself to impose order on that world. I'll wager that you were very young when this happened.

As we grow older we forget that these are not inherent meanings, but the meanings we have chosen. These systems work for us . . . up until the point they don't. Every so often, society likes to smack us across the face and remind us that reality is far more complex than the frameworks we devise to explain it. If you've been using that system since your youth, the loss of it can feel traumatic, like you've had your whole personality ripped away and there's nothing left but a small, defenseless child. But that's not true. It's only your illusions that have been stripped away. You are still you. But in this moment, if you can see that you created these values for yourself, then you can also find the power to change them.

The important thing is to take the time to let this unfold. Don't make any rash decisions. Eventually, after time, I hope that you'll be able to find a way to build a new model, a new set of beliefs, a new version of yourself, a new picture of society, one where morality and justice can be more forgiving.

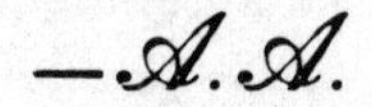

Dear Aunt Antigone:

Our monarch has gone mad. Long ago, he discovered his wife had been unfaithful, so he beheaded her. Now he weds and beds a different woman every night, only to behead that woman in the morning so that he can ensure no one will ever betray him again. This has been going on for years, and nobody yet has found the courage to stand up to the king.

My father is the vizier, and he brought me up to believe in justice, public service, and doing what is right for our people. I cannot bear to let another life be sacrificed to this tyrant's insanity. So, I have volunteered to be his next wife. And I have a plan.

I have read the books, annals, and legends of preceding kings and a thousand histories. I can recite the works of the great poets. I have studied philosophy and the sciences. I am pleasant and I am polite. When the king calls for me, I will ask to see my sister Dunyazad one last time. When she comes, she will ask me to tell her a story. And I will talk. I will spin tales of adventure and excitement, of loves found and lost, of great rulers and evil tyrants. And when I have reached the most dramatic point in the story, I will stop. If he wants to hear the rest, he'll have to wait for the next night. The next night I will do the same. And the night after, and the night after, for as long as I can. And while I do that, no more women will die.

When he found out my plan, my father became enraged and he tried to talk me out of it, telling me that I was throwing my life away. But somebody must do something. Why shouldn't it be me?

—Hanging from the Cliff

Dear Hanging:

One might hope that your level of commitment, self-sacrifice, and honor could be found in the heart of the king himself, but I suppose that would be too much to hope for. When a ruler has overstepped his bounds, committed crimes, or defied the will of the gods, it takes a brave woman to try to stop him. I would be the last person to tell you not to try.

But have pity on your poor father and do not blame him for trying to talk you out of it. It's easy to admire a heroine in the abstract. But when you know them, when they are your flesh and blood, it gets a lot more difficult. And make no mistake, what you are planning is heroic. Whether you are making a noble sacrifice or heralding a triumph is yet to be seen and will depend on whether your skill as a storyteller is as good as you believe it to be. But regardless of the outcome, your intention is noble and pure.

I'm sure you have prepared more than enough stories to enthrall and distract this small-minded misogynist, but have you asked yourself what will happen if you succeed? Will you have to stay married to him indefinitely? Perhaps it's best to not look too far ahead and focus on the danger right in front of you. One impossible problem—and one story—at a time.

Chapter 9

ENDINGS

We all make plans. We all have hopes, dreams, and ambitions. Yet no matter where we come from or how we pursue them, our plans all have one thing in common: they end. Sometimes they end in success, other times they end in failure; life has a way of continually forcing us to change our plans, rewrite them, enlarge or shrink them to meet our everchanging circumstances. And, of course, eventually we all die, and our plans evaporate.

When I was young, I had a head full of plans for my future. I was supposed to see my father preside over a long and prosperous rule. My brothers should have followed him, ruling in harmony. I would have married my beloved, and our children would have taken Thebes into a prosperous future. And as it turned out, none of my plans came to fruition. Sometimes I regret that. Other times, I feel liberated from all the things that weighed on me, all my hopes, fears, and worries for the future. No matter what, I try to accept that things played out in the only way they could. I succeed, most of the time.

Everything eventually ends. But endings often lead to new beginnings.

Dear Aunt Antigone:

My father, Unoka, was a weak man. He did not provide for his family. He was not respected by the community. He died with shame and with many debts. I swore that I would never allow myself to be despised and disrespected as he was. I have built my whole life on that principle. I was strong where he was weak. I am known throughout the nine villages as a wrestling champion and so have provided for my family. Since I reached manhood, I have taken on burdens I didn't want. I did not let my emotions get the better of me, even when I was called on to do the unspeakable. Even when I had to atone for events that were not my responsibility, for actions that I did not commit. I have borne all of these with stoicism.

I have done everything in the opposite of what my father would have done. So why, then, has everything gone wrong? Why have I been exiled? Why has everything fallen apart? Why do I have no more roads in front of me?

Why does my village hate me as much—more—than they ever hated him?

—Always Wrestling Something

Dear Wrestling:

Fathers: When we're young, we think they're gods. As we age, then we think they're tyrants or fools. If we're lucky, we learn that they're just men, fallible as anyone else.

You sound a lot like my father. But trust me, no matter how much your father transgressed against your community's standards, I guarantee you it was nothing compared to what my father did. He too was strong-willed and principled. He took on impossible tasks. He decided that his lot in life was unacceptable, and so he dedicated himself to living a different way. And like you, he found that everything he did to chart a different path only led him back to the very place he was trying to escape from. It did not make him a happy man.

You'd be forgiven for thinking that all life has taught you was that your attempts to change were futile, doomed from the start. But that line of thought won't provide you any solace. So, you might take this opportunity to look more dispassionately at your feelings about your father. When was the moment he went from being your idol to your disappointment? Can you pinpoint what happened? Was it your own decision, or was there a point where you allowed the opinions of the community to supplant your own love for him?

You've spent a lifetime being ashamed of your father. Perhaps at one point that was necessary for you to separate from him, to make yourself your own man. But now that you've had your own experiences of failure, does continuing to blame him give you strength? Could you find it in your heart to forgive him? I urge you to try that, as it may lead you toward forgiving yourself. In the act of forgiveness, you might discover a whole new set of roads open to you, but first it would require finding a way to stop wrestling with your complicated legacy.

Dear Aunt Antigone:

I've done what I had to do. Have I hurt people? Yes. Killed people? Yes. Am I remorseful? No. Does that make me a monster? People have thought that of me for as long as I can remember. But I never let it bother me before.

When I was a little girl, I would often feel like I was surrounded by a forest of enemies. Everyone was out to hurt me and there was nowhere for me to hide. But I learned a trick from reading Alice. *I kept a small bottle in my pocket, filled with sugar water, with a label that said* DRINK ME. *And when I felt like I was trapped, I would drink from the bottle and imagine myself growing smaller, going away, so they couldn't hurt me anymore. But I never drank the whole bottle. I knew if I did, I would disappear completely and cease to exist. I always held a little back. It was my safety net.*

I don't have sugar water anymore. Now I have six grains of morphine in a capsule in a vial hanging from my necklace. I find myself clutching the vial often, unconsciously. It's a comfort. I can still escape. It really might be time to escape. Everything is going sour: My hands hurt from the arthritis. Joe has been conspiring against me. A man was following me for weeks, and when I confronted him, he said he was my son. I could see the face of his father in him. I could see my face too.

I always knew I was different from everyone else. Smarter, stronger. I had something they lacked. But I can't keep Cal's face out of my mind, his cruel smile. Is it possible that I've had it backward all this time? Is it me who's lacking something that everyone else has?

What if the things they all said about me were right? What if I really am an evil monster? What if my soul is malformed?

—Salinas Valley Satanic

Dear Salinas:

Who gets to decide if you are a monster? You, or someone else? Who is the judge here, and who is the jury? From the contents of your vial, I think it's clear who would be the executioner. And who, in this whole metaphorical court you've constructed, is your defense attorney? Who will speak on your behalf? If no one else will, then allow me to.

How exactly does a soul get malformed? Is it from birth? Some chain of heredity or a curse in the blood? Or perhaps it's through adaptation and camouflage. Humans are resourceful creatures, and we can find ways to keep ourselves alive in many adverse, damaging circumstances. When the environment is hostile, life is the first priority, and the comportment of the soul becomes a secondary concern. It certainly sounds like you spent at least some of your childhood immersed in hostility, surrounded by, and running from, enemies. When that happens at a young enough age, we can tend to re-create those enemies for ourselves across the rest of our days, replaying that trauma over and over. Eventually, it can be hard to tell the difference between the trauma and you.

But wait, I can hear your metaphorical prosecutor objecting. "Adverse childhood experiences do not excuse transgressive behavior in an adult!" Yes, that's true. But this isn't a trial about whether or not you've committed crimes. You've confessed to those. The question here is if you are a monster. The question here is about good and evil.

But as much as the moralists want it to be otherwise, evil is not a noun or adjective. Evil is a verb. Evil is something you do, not something you are. To accept the label of monster, to define yourself as a thing that is evil, is just an elaborate way of saying that you couldn't help yourself. In that way, theologians and demonologists conspire to common purpose—to make evil something fixed and unchangeable. There is a certain comfort in that.

The truth is, you're not a monster, and you're not evil. You may have had good reasons and justifiable fears for doing what you've done, but any crimes you've committed were done by your own volition and are your own responsibility. You may be called upon to pay for those crimes. You may choose to punish or exonerate yourself. But it's still up to you.

As long as you draw breath, you may still choose to do good or evil.

Dear Aunt Antigone:

In this war, I've seen a lot of crazy things. But I think it was Snowden that broke me, his guts spilling out of his flak jacket and into my hands. After that, I decided I wasn't going to do it anymore. I was going to live forever or die in the attempt. I did everything I could to avoid flying more missions, but no matter what stunt I pulled, the army kept coming up with new ways to put me back in a plane. It was quite the catch.

Finally, the colonels came up with a deal to get rid of me. They'd send me home. All I had to do was tell everyone they were doing a good job, to be a team player. But I just couldn't do it. I couldn't let them send up some other poor schmuck in my place. So, I decided to run, to take my chances in Rome. But then we learned something impossible happened.

My friend died. Before. He was shot down. I mean, he was always getting shot down, every mission. But this time he didn't come back. And we thought he was dead. But he wasn't. He was alive. Somehow. And he'd rowed all the way to Sweden*! I have no idea how he did it. But he did.*

I'm going to follow in his tracks. I'm leaving as soon as I can. Am I crazy for thinking I can row from Rome *to* Sweden*? If he could do it, why can't I?*

—Contagious Insanity

Dear Contagious:

I may never have been a soldier myself, but I have had firsthand experience of war. My brothers fought on opposite sides of a war, and both were killed. The death and destruction didn't end with them but reverberated out, claiming so many more of us. Any war leader who says they know what will happen is a liar. The only things you can count on in war are madness, injustice, and unintended consequences.

I don't know if you're crazy or not, but if your friend really did row that far before, then there has to be a way for you to do it now. I would just be concerned that you are pursuing a metaphorical ending to your wartime experience by thrusting yourself into an actual war environment. Just because you're not fighting for your country anymore doesn't mean you won't have to fight your way from Rome to Sweden.

Plus, that's a long way to row, all by yourself. Is there someone else who could join you and share the journey and the danger? When there's a real, live, breathing person next to you, suddenly it can become a lot easier and more real to decide what's worth fighting for.

Good luck, and write to me again if you make it.

—A.A.

Dear Aunt Antigone:

I've been imprisoned in my tower for longer than I can remember, by a witch who says she is doing it for my own protection. There are no doors in my room, only a window. Every day when the witch comes to visit, I throw my long blond hair down and she climbs up. I've threatened to cut off my hair so she can't get in anymore, but she only laughs at me and says that I would starve without her.

It was like this for years until one day I heard a different voice calling me to let down my hair. When I did, the person who climbed up was not the witch. He was a prince. I fell in love with him instantly. He comes to me now every day, and the witch has no idea.

Together we've hatched a plan. Every day when he comes, he brings with him a piece of silk, which I use to fashion a rope. Soon, the rope will be long enough for me to climb down and escape forever. It's all I can think about.

And yet, in the midst of my excitement, I am petrified. Sometimes when I look out my tower window, I am seized with panic and dread, and I think to myself that I don't want to leave. But I do *want to go. It's all I've ever wanted. So why am I feeling so conflicted?*

—Blond Ambition

Dear Blond:

What you are feeling is completely natural. You're on the verge of a monumental change. If all you've ever known was the inside of the cell in your tower, it's perfectly understandable to fear what is outside. The idea of escape may be irresistible, but it also comes with a host of practical questions. Where will you live? How will you eat? What happens when it rains? Do you have shoes that hold up in mud? On a larger scale, you're placing a lot of trust in this prince, whom you really don't know all that well. Can you rely on him? What will happen if the witch finds out? Will she chase after you?

But apart from the practicalities, there's a more basic emotional truth to recognize. You are ending a major phase in your life, and no matter how much you are looking forward to the next one, it's natural to have some reticence and fear. You may even need to spend some time grieving the loss of your old way of living, no matter how much you hate it. That's not to approve of your imprisonment or say that it was in any way justified. But it's what you are used to, and as you are about to enter a whole new world of things strange and unfamiliar, it's natural that parts of you will put up some resistance. Every new beginning is also an ending.

Just be careful that in your eagerness to get to your new life or in your grief for the old, you don't accidentally tip off your captor to your plans.

—A.A.

Dear Aunt Antigone:

I never thought I would be the kind of person to sacrifice themselves for someone else. I have always been a disappointment, to myself and everyone else. For the longest time I thought I cared for no one on earth, and no one on earth cared for me. Then I met Lucy. I never knew there could be someone of such love and such light in the world. Of course, I fell in love with her. Unsurprisingly, that love could not be returned.

That her beloved outwardly looked so similar to me was more proof that there was something inherently wrong with my innermost soul. I never expected Lucy to be able to love me. It was enough that she existed in the world, that I could be her friend. That her child could look upon me with something other than hate.

But now, their whole family is in danger. The Revolution wants them dead, and only I can save them. To do so will cost me everything. I do not mind sacrificing my life for her. My life is but a little thing. It gives me no hesitation to throw it away for such a worthy cause.

Only, will it be worth it? Will they remember me? Will one good dead erase a lifetime of waste?

—Chasing the Guillotine

Dear Chasing:

Your life is yours to spend however you choose. I can tell from the self-lacerating words you use that you think you've spent yours poorly. Is that an assessment you have made yourself? Is it someone else's? Why do you think you haven't measured up to expectations, and who's expectations are those?

I read your questions as meaning one of two different things. On the one hand, are you asking me to talk you out of your sacrifice? If that's what you're looking for, then let me tell you this: if you go through with it, you will have to be content with the idea of never knowing if your sacrifice outweighed your past. You'll have to accept that you won't be in any position to make those evaluations. Without knowing for sure if it will pay off, can you still go through with it? Can you live and die without that surety?

On the other hand, if you are firm in your resolve, then the answers to the questions don't really matter. You are the only one who gets to decide the meaning of your sacrifice, and you can make that judgment whenever you choose. However, a word of warning . . .

I know a thing or two about sacrificing everything for your principles. And so I can tell you this: you may feel certain in your decision now, but there will come a moment when you are standing on the brink, when you will realize that there is no way to take it back. Every cell in your body will scream that you have made a mistake. You will castigate yourself as a coward, and every principled choice you have made will seem like idiocy. When this moment comes, don't give in to it. It is not true; it is merely an automatic reaction. It's no reflection on your commitment or your strength. It is a mere fact of biology.

When that moment comes—and believe me, it will come—my advice is to have something to hold on to, something that keeps you true. Hold on tight to it. It will carry you through to the end.

Dear Aunt Antigone:

I've made so many mistakes. I've lost many people dear to me and I stand to lose a lot more. All I can say in my defense is that when the ghost of your murdered father gives you a mission to assassinate the king, I think it's understandable to not leap directly into action. So yes, I was cautious. Even when I was horrible, even when I was wrong, it was always with good intentions. Those intentions don't seem to have counted for much.

I have thought through every decision I have made, analyzed the evidence, examined what conscience and tradition demand, and I've tried to make the best choice at every step of the way in this impossible situation. I've tried to do the right thing.

Before everything went rotten, I studied at the University of Wittenberg. They taught that logic and morality are the keys to wise judgment. That if you look hard enough, you can discern the right signs and signals that allow you to uncover the truth hidden among the lies. You just had to try hard enough, see clearly enough, think deeply enough, and the right choice would become clear. But now it seems that everything I was taught was wrong. I wonder if all of those high-minded ideas are just a way to make yourself feel like you have some kind of control over the world.

They say there is a special providence in the fall of a sparrow. But is there really? Because all the things I've been interpreting as the signs and the signals of providence have turned out to be lies and deceptions. What use are signs at all?

—Friend of Yorick

Dear Friend:

You might be surprised at what I would believe about the pull that fathers have from beyond the grave. And you're right, it sounds like you were put in an impossible position. Anybody would want to slow down, look for additional proof, or more signs of a providential hand before acting on such instructions. Anyone who says otherwise is fooling themselves.

The specific technique you're referring to is called "augury." Nowadays, it's a generic word meaning "omen," but back in my day augury was a very specific craft that involved sacrificing an animal—usually a bird—and reading its entrails to divine the will of the gods or events in the future.

Augury is attractive because it tells you things that you can't see or prove. But there's a reason it fell out of practice—it was unreliable. Random chance meant augurs would be proven right just enough to be seen as maybe credible, but not nearly enough to be bankable. Still, they did a brisk business. Who doesn't want to know the future before it happens? But after a while, people rightly started to wonder if the internal geography of an avian really has any connection to events in the real world. And so, augury fell away, replaced by logic and reason.

Still, reason and augury serve similar functions. They both attempt not only to predict the future before it happens but also to justify past choices, to explain why someone did what they did, and to persuade others that they were in the right. They can quickly become tools in a quest for blamelessness. If what happened was foretold, then aren't you are free of any responsibility for bringing it about?

When you were looking for special providence, for signs and signals, for sparrows, what you were really doing was trying to exert control over your future, while also seeking absolution for your past decisions. This is understandable. We all want control over our lives, and we all want to be able to defend our choices if necessary. But that means we are always living in the past and in the future. Only when we surrender that control, when we let go of the need for justification, can we finally live in the present.

Some people need sparrows, or gods, or philosophies to govern their lives. But you are standing at the brink, ready to let all these things go, surrender to the present, and live in the moment. Can you find a way to stop trying so hard, and just let things be as they are? To let the sparrows fall on their own time?

Dear Aunt Antigone:

I used to want to be alive again. So I tried to go back to my life, but it hurt too much. Now I'm waiting to forget. Mother Gibbs told me that all I had to do was wait, and eventually I'd feel more at home here on the hilltop. But I still miss it sometimes. I miss George and my children and the farm. I miss dresses and coffee. And sleeping. And waking up.

Now we all just lie in our graves, look at the stars, and wait. Nobody really knows why. Nobody really knows for what. Maybe I'm waiting for the earth part of me to burn away, like that Stage Manager says. But I can hear Simon Stimson, and he's still so angry. He hates people because they waste their time, because they're slaves to their self-centered passions. He curses them for their ignorance and blindness. Me, I haven't made up my mind. Maybe I've still got too much of that earth part in me yet.

Do any human beings ever realize life while they live it? Every, every minute? Will we lie here and watch Grover's Corners and the stars forever? Then what?

—Emily Webb (deceased)

Dear Emily:

Every culture has a story to explain what happens after death. Who knows if one of them is right, if all of them are right, or if none of them are right? It's all incomprehensible to our senses. So I'm not sure what will happen to you if and when your "earth part" burns away. But I'll tell you what I think.

I think we're all given a certain amount of time. Short or long. That we spend that time trying to make sense of things as best we can, but we never can come close to getting it all right. And at some point it's all going to end. We'll all march one by one back into the inky nothingness from whence everything came. Every living thing will wink out until the final one goes, and then there will be nothingness, eternally, forever.

I know that might sound grim, but I actually find it quite reassuring because no matter how you count it, no matter the scale, all we get is a brief, wonderful moment. Why not love that moment as much as you can, in any way humanly possible?

Dear Aunt Antigone:

Everything around me is darkness, cold, death. I am here against my will, made to stay due to forces beyond my control.

Here is how I came to be here: one day, I was playing under the bright sun, when the earth split open and a chariot emerged. The charioteer grabbed me and took me to his Underworld kingdom. He placed me on a throne and gave me gold and jewels. His subjects bowed to me as their queen. All the while, I swore and cried and sank into myself. I spent my days walking in circles in the gloomy garden, refusing every offer of food or comfort.

I know that my mother searched everywhere for me. I know that she threatened to destroy everything if she did not get me back. I saw her again for a brief moment before the awful truth came out—once, in the garden, when I was so lost in my grief and anger, I ate something without thinking. Not much. Just a few seeds from the pomegranate tree.

Those seeds doomed me forever. Because of immutable laws that not even Zeus can break, I now must spend several months out of the year here in the Underworld. Each time I return here, it feels like I'm dying all over again. I feel like there is no more hope, that this time will be permanent.

Truly everything is darkness, cold, and death. How do I go on? How do I face another day of this confinement?

—Queen of the Underworld

Your Majesty:

Every so often I recognize the correspondent behind the pseudonym. Generally, I don't acknowledge it, lest it distract from the matter at hand. But in this case, I am compelled to make an exception. For you have always been kind to me, and we have some things in common. I have prayed to you, and for you, and think of you every time I eat a pomegranate.

You may be a goddess, but you are still bound by some of the same strictures that bind mortals. And so I'll advise you the same thing I would advise any other who asked the same question.

You go on. You just do. You find any way you can to get through the day. Maybe that's singing a song in the face of catastrophe. Maybe it's keening your grief for all to hear. Maybe it's getting right up in the face of your husband and screaming at him until your voice is raw. Maybe it's walking in a circle around that pomegranate tree in the garden seventeen million times. Maybe it's playing fetch with Cerberus. Try anything. Try everything.

All you have to do is survive this moment. And then the next. And then the next. It may seem impossible. It may feel like it's tearing your soul apart. But one day, you will look up, and the sun will be shining again. You will emerge from your captivity and go into the light. And the whole world will come back to life.

Just hold on until then. You can do it. I believe in you.

—A.A.

AFTERWORD

While I was writing this book, the entire world changed.

I got a late start due to a minor surgery and the subsequent recovery period. When I finally sat down to start working at the start of February 2020, I tried to block out all other concerns. And then the pandemic hit.

COVID-19 didn't change much for me at first. If anything, I found that sheltering-in-place afforded me more writing time, fewer interruptions. While everyone else I knew was having their lives upended, my days stayed pretty much the same—get up, sit down, write, and try to ignore the internet.

Then my father got sick.

There was a morning when I sat down to work, consumed with worry for him, unable to get started. And the thought came to me that right then, the person who needed Aunt Antigone's advice more than anyone else was *me*. So I wrote to her myself:

Dear Aunt Antigone:

As I have been going through this process of writing your book, I have come to marvel at how, even though all of your thoughts and opinions and advice flow out through my own hands, nevertheless you feel like a separate personality. You are more confident, more assured, firmer, and I dare say a little kinder than I am—certainly in the advice you give to some people to whom I would be much harsher.

For example, our journey together began when I was first asked to write some sample entries and considered the problem of Scarlett O'Hara. I would have liked to tell her to get over herself, to feel shame at the enormous wealth that she possessed through obscene and criminal means, that her problems were laughable, inane, meaningless on the scale of the suffering that was happening around her. But you would not permit that. You took her at her word, and tried to see through her eyes, even while framing parts of the larger context in a gentle way that perhaps she'd be able to make sense of through her own limited perspective.

Right now, our book deadline is a week away, and a slow-motion apocalypse is spreading across the world. Every day brings new warnings and desperate measures to slow the coronavirus, and we're under a stay-at-home order. A few days ago, I spoke to my mother and learned that my father has had a fever for several days. His doctor told her to send him to the hospital. They live in New Jersey, on the other side of the country from me, although even if we'd been in the same town there'd be nothing I could have done. All I could do was keep working.

I had one of the most productive writing days of the entire project. I buried my perspective into yours and tried to think of nothing else. Late in the day, I got the news that they were releasing him. His fever had gone down, they gave him antibiotics and sent him home with instructions to rest and monitor his temperature.

The next day, I was a wreck. I was now paying for all of the focus I'd had while waiting for news. I managed to push through just a couple of entries—Mathilde from "The Necklace" and poor, deluded, overthinking Raskolnikov from Crime and Punishment.

The next week was full of phone calls, hourly temperature checks, a color-coded spreadsheet to track his condition. Yesterday, I awoke to the news that my mother had trouble rousing him in the morning. But when he finally woke up, his temperature was down to 99 and he had an appetite for the first time in over a week. I was finally able to speak to him. He sounded exhausted, but clearheaded. I told him I loved him. He told me that he was looking forward to reading this book.

It felt like we'd all dodged a bullet. I sat down to write a few more entries. Next up were Long John Silver from Treasure Island *and someone from* A Christmas Carol. *Initially I'd hoped to do something with Jacob Marley—the recent TV reimagining with the great Stephen Graham playing an expanded version of the role was still fresh in my mind—but a review of the text didn't seem to support the idea. I briefly considered using Bob Cratchit but ultimately decided that for a section about money, there was no way to avoid the big man, ol' Ebenezer Scrooge himself. I started rereading the opening. "Marley was dead: to begin with. There is no doubt whatever about that."*

A text came in from my mother. My father's temperature had suddenly spiked again. He was shivering uncontrollably. His breathing was labored. The doctor told her that they couldn't avoid it any longer. An ambulance was on the way to take him back to the hospital.

That was an hour ago. No more news has come through. I'm terrified. I'm sitting here, trying to write about loveless, friendless, utterly alone Scrooge, trying to imagine how you'd try to reach him. And I realized that in this moment I need your advice a lot more than Ebenezer does.

Do I still try to keep working while I wait for news? If I stop working, and the worst happens, I fear that I won't be able to start again.

—The Author, March 30, 2020

When I finished writing the letter, I just kept going, doing what I'd done for all the others. I wrote her reply. To my surprise, I realized that she was giving me the start of the book's afterword.

Dear Jay:

If you keep working, that's okay. If you don't keep working, that's okay too. You have an entire support system that will help you finish this book, so don't spare a thought about it right now, and don't worry about not being able to start writing again. If you were able to once find refuge in the work, you will so again.

And you won't have to do any of this alone. You have an entire crackerjack team behind you at Tiller Press, led by Veronica Alvarado, your incredible editor, who will make sure that this book is everything you want it to be, and Michael Andersen, who initially pitched the concept to you, who will be tickled at the secret hidden in the Lovecraft passage, and who you will eventually convince to write a history of Alternate Reality Games. You have countless friends who support you—more than you think—on Slack boards, through text messages, on Zoom calls, and all the other ways to express love and care while sheltering in place.

You have Bronwen, your wife and partner. You love her. She knows.

You have your mother, Jessie, and your sister, Dana, who are carrying this with you. And you have your father, Dave, who will *read this book, who will get the very first copy.*

And you have me. I'm not going to let you down. No matter what happens, I'll keep going.

I know you're waiting for that Hamlet *entry that's going to come in the final chapter. I know that's the one you've been holding to the end as a reward for writing all the others. Let me remind you again of the passage that you love, that unlocked everything else:*

"Not a whit. We defy augury. There's a special providence in the fall of a sparrow. If it be now, 'tis not to come. If it be not to come, it will be now. If it be not now, yet it will come—the readiness is all."

Don't predict what might or might not happen. Don't think too far into the future. Stick with what is right in front of you right now, what you are experiencing in this moment, whatever that needs to be. If that's writing Scrooge, fine. If not, that's fine too. The readiness is all. Defy augury. Hold your father in your heart, and whatever happens, you will be ready for it.

–A.A.

Writing to Antigone helped. Scrooge got done, and then the rest.

After a day of oxygen therapy in the hospital, my father was put on a ventilator. I submitted the final chapters of the book on April 3.

On April 5, he died.

The following week passed in a dream. I wrote his obituary. We watched a shaky Facetime of his casket being lowered into his grave. We held a memorial on Zoom, a three-hour call where over a hundred people shared their memories about him. I tried to get used to speaking about him in the past tense.

As I listened to all the stories and told my own, a new thought came to me. The characters in this book are all fictional, their problems bounded by the stories they come from. But one day, each of us will be gone, and all that will be left of us will be the memories and tales that others remember. And then the difference between real and fictional won't matter anymore. We will all be stories.

A few months ago, in a different lifetime, I told my dad that I'd be writing this book. He was excited and proud. I was still in the process of choosing all the characters, and he sent me some suggestions. One stood out as a great idea, which I immediately adopted: Yossarian from *Catch-22*. I hadn't read the book in years, but I did recall my dad, a long time ago, telling me about seeing a piece of graffiti that he'd never forgotten. Someone had spray-painted on a wall, YOSSARIAN IS ALIVE AND WELL AND LIVING IN SWEDEN. It was the sort of joke he loved, one that riffed on a piece of pop culture while celebrating independence, subversion, and hope.

Aunt Antigone was wrong about one thing. My father will never get to hold a copy of this book. But she was right about everything else, about the oceans of support that poured out. Some of those names she listed above, but there are a few more people I need to mention who have helped me throughout the life of this book and with so many other things:

My writing group, the Shamers, who never cease to inspire me. I am awed by your talents, and even more by your hearts. Everyone from the Creative's Workshop, especially the Magpies and the Otters, for showing up with generosity. And a special thank-you to Jennifer Hole for Louisa Musgrove.

My friend and fellow Cloudmaker, Andrea Phillips, whose "Madame Zee" was certainly an influence. I like to image Madame Zee and Aunt Antigone having tea together and calling each other "dear" a lot. Sara Thacher, who gave me my first chance to write as an agony aunt as part of the *Ghost Post.* I tried to fit Tireseas in, but it turned out to be a hat on top of a hat.

The folks on all my myriad Slack boards: the Evans Chan, Social-D, the I.D.L. squad, Jedi Master Noah Nelson and all the merry lunatics from the No Proscenium community. Anybody who's ever taken part in an argument about what the word *transmedia* means.

Michael McConnell at Zero Gravity Management. Matt Sugarman and Jamie Lincenberg at Weintraub Tobin. At Tiller Press: Shelly Perron, for the discovery that copyediting can be a fun scavenger hunt. Patrick Sullivan, for that amazing cover design that I've seen make so many faces light up. Designer Jenny Chung and production editor Laura Jarrett—if my words are lousy, at least they'll look smashing thanks to you.

Barrett Garese, for all the virtual hugs. David Nett, for always having my nerdy back. Dan Goldman, for being a super-mensch. Megan Westerby: Play the drum so your mom can see you on TV.

To all of you, and all the others who have been there, I am eternally grateful.

For my father, Dave Bushman. June 1, 1943–April 5, 2020. I'll see you in Sweden one day.

—Jay Bushman, April 17, 2020

ABOUT THE AUTHOR

JAY BUSHMAN writes for many kinds of media. For over a decade, Jay has worked at the intersection of traditional and emerging formats, reinterpreting and reimagining classic stories in new ways.

Jay won an Emmy for his work as a writer and transmedia producer on the groundbreaking series *The Lizzie Bennet Diaries*, an interactive adaptation of Jane Austen's *Pride and Prejudice*. He wrote one of the first Twitter novels, "The Good Captain," an adaptation of Herman Melville's "Benito Cereno," for which one publication dubbed him "The Epic Poet of Twitter." One of these days he's really going to get that printed up on business cards.

Jay lives and works in Los Angeles.